# Post Conflict Sri Lanka: Rebuilding of the Society

# Post Conflict Sri Lanka: Rebuilding of the Society

*Edited by*
**V. R. Raghavan**

**Vij Books India Pvt Ltd**
New Delhi (India)

Published by

**Vij Books India Pvt Ltd**

2/19, Ansari Road, Darya Ganj
New Delhi - 110002
Phones: 91-11-47340674, 91-11- 43596460
Fax: 91-11-47340674
e-mail   : vijbooks@rediffmail.com
web : www.vijbooks.com

**Centre for Security Analysis**
"9-B" Ninth Floor,
Chesney Nilgiri, 71, Ethiraj Salai,
Egmore, Chennai-600008
Tamil Nadu, India
+91-44-65291889
office@csa-chennai.org
www.csa-chennai.org

**First Published : 2012**

**ISBN**      **: 978-93-81411-32-2**

# Table of Contents

# Acknowledgements

The Centre for Security Analysis (CSA) has undertaken a three year research project **Internal Conflicts and Transnational Consequences** supported by the John D and Catherine T MacArthur Foundation. This volume is part of the ongoing project and its publication has been possible by the project grant.

The Editor places on record the assistance and support provided by Prof Amal Jayawardane, Executive Director, Regional Centre for Security Studies (RCSS), Colombo in organising the seminar on which this book is based.

# Foreword

The Centre for Security Analysis (CSA) focusses on widening the perspective of security discourse beyond military and traditional aspects, to include non–traditional dimensions such as food, environment, energy, water, political and societal security. To achieve this objective, CSA endeavours to build awareness on these issues through public discourse and contributes to the policy formulation by making available, analyses and studies, to the policy planners as well as involving them in the discourse.

CSA, in collaboration with think tanks in Sri Lanka, has organised studies and seminars over the years to address the internal conflict in Sri Lanka, at its various stages. CSA aims to provide a platform to develop a discourse which is inclusive of the conflict's stakeholders. Over 60 experts, including ministers and senior bureaucrats of the Government of Sri Lanka, economists, social scientists, media, civil society representatives and other distinguished analysts and think tank members from India and Sri Lanka put forth their perspectives at these seminars. These have been published in edited volumes listed below:

- Conflict in Sri Lanka: Internal and External Consequences

- From Winning the War to Winning Peace: Post War Rebuilding of the Society in Sri Lanka

- Conflict in Sri Lanka: The Road Ahead

- Peace Process in Sri Lanka: Challenges & Opportunities

- Federalism and Conflict Resolution in Sri Lanka

- Conflict Resolution and Peace Building in Sri Lanka

- Conflict over Fisheries in the Palk Bay Region

The end of the three decades' old armed conflict in Sri Lanka not only brings a new era of hope and optimism to millions of Sri Lankans which they truly deserve, it also poses formidable challenges to the Government of Sri Lanka in the nation building process. A number of studies conducted about post conflict recoveries in Asia, Africa and Latin America have provided ideas, strategies and examples of good practices on the post conflict reconciliation process. Interestingly, these studies have also highlighted that the fundamental principle in all the post conflict activities is the *context*. Sri Lanka is no exception in this regard. Developing infrastructure and building institutions and providing inputs for economic activities alone do not achieve long lasting peace and durable reconciliation. Therefore, developmental strategies in Sri Lanka should be considered and shaped, keeping in view, the local context which would include the political system, socio-economic practices and ethnic, linguistic and religious divergence. It is also worthwhile remembering the causes of the conflict, conflict characteristics and consequences of the conflict which tend to shape the path of recovery. While strategising the post developmental plans, it is essential to reverse and transform the adverse conditions that caused the conflict. It is also essential to reduce the risk of the conflict recurrence.

Sri Lanka has made remarkable progress in the spheres of immediate humanitarian assistance and resettlement of IDPs, de-mining, reconstruction of infrastructure, rehabilitation of ex-combatants, restoration of law & order and democratic institutions / instruments and initiatives of long term economic development projects. The programs being implemented, do certainly address the basic material needs of the conflict affected people, mostly in the North and East of the country. However, other non- material human needs like security and the recognition of the identity are also of equal existential importance. If these are neglected, the studies have shown that the affected populace tends to express its disappointment in ethnic terms. The ultimate aim of the post conflict strategy is to re-establish the conditions for self-sustaining economic growth and human development. These include addressing group inequalities (generally referred to as *Horizontal Inequalities* by researchers), ethnic diversity, peace and well being of the local populace and their institutions.

Rebuilding of the society involves much more than reconstruction of infrastructure and economic development. It also requires reconciliation. Although local government elections were held and peoples' representatives have been elected for the grass root level management, a fully fledged political reconciliation has not been realised yet. Without reconciliation, it would be difficult to lay the foundation for a vibrant nation. Reconciliation may appear far more difficult to achieve after a painful and protracted conflict. However there are many promising conditions and also great potential which should be harnessed. Reconciliation is a cooperative effort and involves many stakeholders.

In this context I would like to draw attention to a debate that took place in the Indian Parliament on the post-conflict rebuilding process in Sri Lanka. There was great appreciation for the efforts that were carried out by the Government of Sri Lanka. Mr. S. M. Krishna, External Affairs Minister, made a statement on the floor of the house "… While the Government of India is of the view that the end of conflict in Sri Lanka provides an opportunity to pursue a lasting political settlement in Sri Lanka, within the framework of a united Sri Lanka, acceptable to all the communities in Sri Lanka including the Tamils, it has to be kept in mind that this is a long standing issue and Sri Lanka is going through its internal processes, including structured dialogue between the Government and representatives of Tamil parties. The sooner Sri Lanka can come to a political arrangement within which all the communities feel comfortable and which works for all of them, the better. In this context, the commencement of a structured dialogue on pursuing a political solution for national reconciliation as well as reconstruction and development, is a laudable development. We will do whatever we can to support this process." [1] There has been a sea change both in India and Sri Lanka, on the issue of political reconciliation.

At this juncture, it is worthwhile to reflect on achievements, shortfalls and gaps and take stock of the current state of affairs, look closely at some of the variables that would speed up the post war rehabilitation, reconstruction

[1] Suo Moto Statement in Lok Sabha & Rajya Sabha by Shri S. M. Krishna, External Affairs Minister on "The Situation in Sri Lanka", 4 August 2011

and rebuilding and explore as to how these processes can be made sustainable and lasting.

To address these issues, CSA engaged a number of experts from India and Sri Lanka to carry out research on the themes – managing political challenges in rebuilding the society, socio-economic challenges and challenges of harmonising ethnic diversity. These research papers were presented at a seminar "Post Conflict Sri Lanka: Rebuilding of the Society" organised in Colombo. Prof Tissa Vitharana, senior minister of Scientific Affairs delivered the key note address. He is a person who has been deeply concerned about the ramifications of the ethnic problem in the country long before he became a key minister in the Government of Sri Lanka. Former Indian Ambassador, G. Parthasarthy and Sri Lankan Ambassador, Javid Yusuf gave their perspectives on the issue.

This volume will be of much interest to policy planners, academia and all those concerned with the post conflict activities in Sri Lanka.

V. R. Raghavan

# 1 | Introduction

K Srinivasan and Ancy Joseph

The ethnic conflict that devastated Sri Lanka over a period of three decades ended in May 2009 with the defeat of LTTE. The absence of armed conflict does not necessarily mean that peace and stability have been attained. Protracted conflict leads to immeasurable loss in terms of human and physical infrastructure; it also leads to the collapse of systems and institutions thus rendering society dysfunctional. Post conflict states face formidable social, economic and political challenges, hence needing an effective and holistic approach to rebuilding and reconstructing the state. A candid assessment of prevailing conditions of post–conflict state will help in formulating the post conflict recovery program as post-conflict reconstruction issues are linked to the specific challenges each country has to overcome. Political leadership, level of democratisation, presence of democratic institutions, capacities of civil administration, state of economic growth, ethnic composition etc. are important factors that have great impact on the post conflict rebuilding efforts.[1] In a pluralistic society, reconciliation becomes very crucial in achieving lasting peace and stability. Therefore rebuilding efforts should involve all stakeholders, at all stages.

The Sri Lankan conflict was extremely violent, protracted and costly both in terms of human and physical destruction. The end of fighting has offered Sri Lanka an opportunity to work towards lasting peace and security

---

[1] " Governance Strategies for Post Conflict Reconstruction , Sustainable Peace and Development", UN DESA Discussion Paper - GPAB/REGOPA Cluster, Division of Public Administration and Development Management, November 2007 available online at http://unpan1.un.org/intradoc/groups/public/documents/un/unpan028332.pdf

for the entire population. Immediately after the end of the war, Sri Lanka's efforts were essentially focussed on resettlement of internally displaced people (IDPs) and de-mining of the conflict area. Sri Lanka has achieved tremendous successes in connection with the reconstruction effort. A large number of international organisations assisted Sri Lanka in this challenging endeavour. The Government of India extended material and financial support for rebuilding fifty thousand houses besides other infrastructure development activities in various fields like the airport, seaport, power and railways. Sri Lankan government has embarked on widespread rehabilitation and reconstruction with two ambitious programs, namely "*Uthuru Wasanthaya*" (Northern Spring)" and "*Negenahira Navodya*" (Eastern Rising) targeted at poverty reduction and socio-economic development in the war ravaged areas. Other supplementary programs at regional and village level have also been initiated.

Against this backdrop, the Centre for Security Analysis organised a seminar to reflect on the achievements, shortfalls and look at some of the variables that would speed up the post war rehabilitation, reconstruction and rebuilding processes and explore as to how these processes can be made sustainable and lasting. Nine experts from India and Sri Lanka addressed various facets of the post conflict rebuilding challenges. A brief of the view points of the researchers are given in the following paragraphs.

In his key note address, Senior Minister Tissa Vitharana, lauds the government's work in areas of rehabilitation and reconstruction but points out that no reconstruction process is complete without arriving at a political solution to the ethnic issue. He observes that diversity is Sri Lanka's strength but unfortunately this diversity has been used to its disadvantage, by having caused conflict situations to arise. All Party Representatives Committee (APRC) which he chaired, identified twenty one political issues that needed to be addressed to work out a political solution to the ethnic problem. The APRC process lasted three years, had 126 sittings and came up with a consensus among thirteen party representatives, on twenty one political issues that required agreement. Five issues were incorporated into the second political manifesto of the President. Thereafter, the APRC process was discontinued. But other processes were set in motion to find a solution to the ethnic issue. A dialogue between the Government and Tamil National

Alliance started and also a Select Committee of Parliament, with representatives of all political parties, was set up. But no significant progress has been made. One of the facts that emerged during the APRC process was that, a federal solution that the TNA had been advocating for, would not materialise. TNA won the local government elections in North Province, crushing the expectations of the incumbent government that economic and development programs were enough to garner the support of the Tamils. The Sinhala Buddhist and Tamil separatist lobbies acted as spoilers in the process of seeking political solution. The public outcry of the international community and the diaspora on human rights violations put the Sri Lankan Government on the defensive and made the task of finding a political solution very difficult. He is of the opinion that a solution based on devolution can be achieved despite opposing views within the government and outside; however a conducive atmosphere needs to be generated both within and outside the country. His views are candid; they explain the complexity of the issues involved and the need for compromise by all stakeholders to find amicable and workable solutions.

In his paper, "Emerging Trends in Indian Regional Policies and Approach to Relations with Sri Lanka" *G Parthasarathy* recounts foreign and security policies of India as an emerging power, particularly with Sri Lanka. India has made sustained efforts for economic integration, not only in South Asia, but also in East and Southeast Asia. The end of the ethnic conflict in Sri Lanka opens new vistas for enhancing bilateral and regional cooperation between India and Sri Lanka. India's ties with Sri Lanka have strengthened on the basis of growing and mutually beneficial trade and economic relations. India views Sri Lanka as a country whose past performance and potential for rapid economic growth make Sri Lanka a reliable and long term partner for bilateral and regional economic cooperation and integration. India has been deeply concerned about the welfare and well being of internally displaced Tamils and extended financial and material support to rehabilitate them. Despite the international pressure on Sri Lanka, for excesses by its army, India maintains a stand that promotes national reconciliation in Sri Lanka. Parthasarathy calls for an innovative framework to resolve the ethnic issue and draws the example of Northern Ireland, where the political situation was addressed within the framework of what is a unitary State.

According to *Rajiva Wijesingha* in his paper "Political Challenges: A Sri Lankan Perspective", the greatest challenge in the post conflict Sri Lanka is restoration of trust between the two communities. Tamils are apprehensive of demographic change and militarisation in the North and East Provinces while the Sinhalese fear domination by a minority through disproportionate influence on governance. He toured the North & East provinces and interacted with the resettled people and found that that the Tamil fears are unwarranted. Given the security concerns, the level of the military presence cannot be scaled down. However, he says it is important for the government to understand the concerns of Tamils and act expeditiously to avoid developing any sense of alienation. Therefore, he recommends recruiting more minorities into the security forces, not only the police but also the army and the other services. He says that the apprehensions of the Sinhalese can be assuaged by ensuring quality educational facilities throughout the island. The government needs to involve the diaspora to work in tandem with government agencies, to improve the situation of minorities. Little effort has been made by the government, thus far, to channelise the energies of members of the diaspora. He is of the view that involvement of the minorities in post conflict development efforts would help dispel the fears and apprehensions. He suggests reforms that will help improve governance- a) bicameral legislature that allows a greater voice to rural areas through a second chamber based on equal representation for all provinces; b) provincial government with an executive that has decision making powers with regard to issues that do not pertain to security or national policy or inter-provincial issues and c) local government with administrative power to take decisions with regard to day to day issues, including social services and utilities. This structure of governance will help uphold the spirit of the 13th amendment, adding greater responsiveness to the people, greater responsibility to the various tiers of government and greater involvement at all levels of the people and their representatives.

In his paper, "Political Challenges: A Tamil Perspective", *K Sarveswaran* expresses strong anti-Sinhala sentiments. He passionately delves into the historical background of the Tamil-Sinhala animosity. He examines pre-war and post-war challenges of Tamil nationalism. He identifies the issue of power sharing and meeting the urgent humanitarian needs of the war victims as challenges in the post war Sri Lanka. Due to international compulsions, the Government of Sri Lanka feigns interest in power sharing and devolution but in reality, many of the top leaders have taken an anti-devolution stand. He writes, though the government has embarked on several developmental projects, the Tamils have not benefitted from these and data given out by different government departments and agencies are far from true. He also criticizes militarisation in the Northern and Eastern regions of the state. The high level of militarisation in the Northern Province has brought forth several problems to the Tamils-a culture of impunity within the military, breakdown of social fabric, assaults on women, involvement of military in dispute settlement, etc.

*Javid Yusuf* in his paper, "A National Perspective through Muslim Eyes" points out that the Muslims are uncertain as to how actions taken by the Sri Lankan State in addressing Tamil grievances will affect them. This has been the perennial dilemma facing the Muslims even during the war period. Muslims strode a separate political path opting to engage with the State and work within the mainstream of Sri Lankan politics. This resulted in a great deal of misunderstanding by the Tamils, of the Muslims strategy and caused a strain in relationships between the two communities. Muslims, despite not being direct protagonists in the armed conflict between the LTTE and the Sri Lankan State, have undergone considerable suffering during the years of fighting in the North and East. He is of the opinion that LTTE made a strategic mistake by resorting to armed struggle to achieve their goals; any attempt at a 'quick fix' of complex political problems cannot arrive at a sustainable solution. The armed struggle has cost the Tamils dearly; Tamil society has been brutalised, Tamil culture has been destroyed and the LTTE's intolerance of dissent and democracy has weakened the proud intellectual spirit of Tamil society. Therefore, in post war environment, it is necessary for the Tamil community to engage in serious introspection with regard to their role and place in Sri Lanka and the strategies they need to adopt to ensure their rightful place in the rebuilding of the country. Sensitivity to fears and apprehensions of the Tamil community, even if at times considered misplaced or exaggerated, becomes imperative to achieving peace and stability. Hence, the Sri Lankan State needs to dispel these fears through concerted efforts. Higher number of army personnel in higher levels of administration in North and East, as well as its intense visible presence at ground-level is not conducive for creating an environment of reintegration and reconciliation. If the security situation leaves no option but the presence of the Army in the region, it must then recede to the background for the present and eventually work towards withdrawal from the region in a phased manner.

In his paper "Socio-economic challenges of Post Conflict Reconstruction in Sri Lanka" *Saman Kelegama* gives a broad overview of the challenges faced by Sri Lanka in the post conflict context. Sri Lanka has been experiencing high growth during the past few years and this opened up new opportunities for improving the economy of the country. Development of Northern and Eastern region play a very crucial role in this regard. The government of Sri Lanka has initiated a number of developmental programs aimed at reducing the poverty and to bring the economy back on track. Saman Kelegama highlights that education is an integral part of the social reconstruction efforts. Sri Lanka's investment in education is lowest among the middle income countries. Therefore, the government should spend more on education not only to educate those in the conflict affected areas, but also to improve the quality of education in Sri Lanka as a whole. The ex-child combatants need special attention and adequate resources should be provided to ensure psycho-social well being. Sri Lanka has been able to maintain overall health indicators at a satisfactory level despite its economic downturns over time. There are major challenges associated with rebuilding hospitals and other health related infrastructure as construction of these buildings often takes a long period of time. Thus, these projects may not meet the health needs of the population in the present. Significant changes need to be made in the country's health systems in order to successfully manage new epidemiological challenges resulting from the return of IDPs. While discussing about challenges of the agriculture sector, he points out that the war has hindered agricultural growth in the North and East. Given the high incidence of poverty among agricultural workers, development in agriculture is very important to the goal of poverty alleviation. The introduction of cutting edge technology in agriculture is required. The improvement of market linkages and relaxation of barriers is desirable in order to induce growth in the agriculture sector. The post conflict environment has increased opportunities for industrialisation. The current policy framework emphasises on small and medium enterprise sectors. A number of export processing zones and industrial estates are being established throughout the country to expand the industrial base. Though many programs exist to address the challenges, there is no integrated strategy to address the issues to generate more inclusive growth. Public financing has proven challenging, given that the tight fiscal constraints and foreign assistance is focussed on infrastructure development. He advocates for private sector participation in education and health sector and those involving Tamil Diaspora in Northern and Eastern regions.

*S B Divaratne,* in his paper, "Resettlement and Development in Northern Sri Lanka: Conflict to Stability" explores the programs and challenges faced by the Sri Lankan government's reconstruction and rehabilitation efforts in the Northern Province. De-mining and restoration of basic infrastructure in order to ensure safe and resettlement programs have been enormous challenges to the government. A Presidential Task Force for Resettlement, Development and Security in the Northern Province (PTF) was appointed in May 2009, which set up a road map to formulate a strategic framework for rapid resettlement and recovery program. The PTF developed a three-pronged approach for resettlement and development- a) providing humanitarian assistance for the resettled people and restoration of basic infrastructure in the cleared area; b) early recovery process to support returnees to recommence their economic activities; c) pursuing the parallel development of much needed major infrastructure and to revive the Northern Region towards sustainability and stability. The biggest contribution made by the GOSL in post conflict reconstruction efforts was in the field of de-mining operation. Humanitarian De-mining Unit (HDU) under Sri Lanka Army was set up and has done commendable work in de-mining. Prior to commencement of the resettlement, the GOSL spearheaded the rapid rehabilitation of infrastructure through its 180-day Program. A Joint Plan for Assistance for the Northern Province was prepared by GOSL in 2010, for assistance needed during 2011. The objective of the JPA was to identify the balance priority activities that must be undertaken during 2011 and facilitate international assistance in order that the people of Northern Province can recover, rebuild and return to a normal life. Economic and social infrastructure development is another element of the strategy for reconstruction of the Northern Province. A massive investment, both external and internal, has been set apart for reconstruction of highways, railways, irrigation network, power supply, water supply etc. The author has provided extensive data on the reconstruction work sourced from government departments.

*N Manoharan* in his paper, "Ethnicity and Nation Building: Lessons from South Asia and Beyond" explicates various theoretical interpretations of the concepts- ethnicity and nation building. Nation building is a continuous but very complex process, particularly in a pluralistic society. State building which involves the creation and development of the institutions of the political system is an integral component of nation building. The character of nation building depends, by and large, on the manner in which a new state is born. In most post colonial countries in South Asia and Africa, state building precedes nation building. To protect themselves against any threats to their security, unity, sovereignty and territorial integrity became their top priority. Therefore, state rather than nation-building was given utmost primacy. Most of the problems in ethnic relations arise because of the failure or biased nature of existing/old institutions. Therefore, the first and foremost requisite in the nation building process is the provision of functioning state institutions, but that are seen as fair, by all communities. Those countries that are emerging from conflicts especially need better institutions just to avoid repetition of old predicaments. He explains two approaches - reconstruction and deconstruction - of institution building in the post conflict context. Under the reconstruction approach, national building process works within the existing institutions and deals, more or less impartially, with all social forces and power centres and redirects their ongoing competition for power and prosperity from violent to peaceful channels. In the deconstruction approach, the existing state apparatus is dismantled and a new one is rebuilt. But the problem arises when these methods are adapted to suit interests of particular communities or individuals in power. The solution to this problem can be 'administrative consociationalism" where processes of accommodation are especially visible in ethnically divided societies, where quotas are sometimes used in the distribution of public offices. India is a classic case of such accommodation where there are multiple quotas. This affirmative action model from India may suit other countries, especially Sri Lanka, where instead of getting into controversial devolution of powers to geographical areas like provinces or districts, one can consider communities as units of devolution. He also examines the role of the constitution, form of governance, electoral system and political parties in nation building. Establishing the balance between retribution and reconciliation in societies emerging from conflict, presents a particular challenge. He asserts that 'civic nationalism' is a critically important factor for nation-building since it fosters a shared public culture and supports meaningful participation in the activities of the state. Appropriate power sharing arrangements limit the authority of the majority and provide guarantees to the development of the minority communities. In divided societies, public services may contribute to the maintenance of a delicate balance between groups. However, nation building in countries can be successful with visionary leadership, inclusive political institutions that respect the fact that minority sentiments exist, good and equal economic development and open, tolerant and forward-looking society. While addressing the majority-minority relations, he aptly rules out 'assimilation'. Instead 'accommodation' alone can bring out unity and cohesion.

In her paper "Challenges to Harmonising Ethnic Diversity", *Gnana Moonesinghe* writes that the task of harmonising ethnic diversity is a complex process involving the implementation of several strategies, programs and structures that will facilitate the creation of trust and confidence amongst the multi-ethnic polity, for unity and the development of a national identity. The sharp ethnic divisions of the 1950's ethos have toned down. She attributes the ethnic divisiveness to misinterpretation of historical facts. The Official Language Act and Buddhism, as a state religion introduced a sense of parochialism to the nation state while de-secularisation of the state removed one of the liberal features of the constitution and raised issues of equity within the mult i- religious polity. Also, making Buddhism a populist base for politics and political manoeuvres gradually eroded much of the essence of Buddhism, the great qualities of compassion, of tolerance and of humility. On the other hand, the Tamil leadership has for the most part continued with the emotive drive for language and culture and identity rights as features of Tamil solidarity. The Tamil Diaspora must become proactive in the reconciliation process and refrain from espousing the cause of Eelam as it is detrimental to the confidence and trust building environment. She examines the role of media as peace builders. Exploring the role of civil society in the nation building process, she writes that mass mobilisation and empowerment of civil society has to be undertaken to enthuse the citizens towards a future in a plural society. The citizens working in their own communities should shoulder the responsibility of taking the peace process forward. She also emphasises the need for compromise in finding solutions and resolute leadership to push forward the peace process.

*N Selvakkuramaran* in his paper, "Harmonising Ethnic Diversity: Linguistic Challenges", looks at the role of language and related issues that formed the basis of discrimination and a reason for the Tamil demand for more autonomy. The first legislative blow to the linguistic equality recognised in and guaranteed by the Independence Constitution, came to pass when the Parliament, soon after the General Election in 1956, passed the Official Language Act which was popularly referred to as the *Sinhala Only Act*. The events that took place thereafter in the country made the Government enact the Tamil Language (Special Provisions) Act in 1958 but Tamil language was not accorded the status of Official Language nor were the people whose mother tongue was Tamil, given the same rights as those whose mother tongue was Sinhala. Pursuant to the Indo-Sri Lanka Accord, the 13th Amendment was enacted to the Second Republican Constitution. It amended Article 18 of the Constitution that dealt with the Official Language of the country. Article 18 introduced also a new concept of 'link language' in the country without any explanation as to its significance or implications. There was a clear inconsistency between the amended Article 18 and other Articles in the Chapter on Language and the failure to amend the other constitutional provisions on Language and to bring them in line with the newly given status of the Tamil language, left room for lack of clarity. The 16th Amendment in 1988 introduced several changes to the then prevailing position on languages. Thereafter administrative convenience and political expediency have been dictating the incremental 'grant' of language rights to the linguistic minorities in the country. Political opportunism and administrative expediency have been the main reasons for the present parlous state of the implementation of linguistic rights of the minorities. Although successive governments have taken steps to address the concerns of linguistic rights of all people in the country through statutory and constitutional enactments, with regard to the use of languages, the implementation of these policy pronouncements has not been effectively and efficiently carried through. The main reason for the inefficient and ineffective implementation of the Official Languages Policy is the fact that the National Policy on Recruitment to the Public/Provincial/Judicial Service and the National Policy on Education/Higher Education do not go hand in hand with the Official Languages Policy. Unless there is a concerted effort to synchronise these three in order to work towards achieving a common objective, the lack of proper implementation will continue to bewilder this country. That will, in turn, make the task of harmonising ethnic diversity in this country, a distant reality and a perpetual challenge.

Reconstruction and rebuilding of the society has to be carried out in tandem with the aspirations of all the stakeholders. Issues need to be discussed amongst all stakeholders, to listen to each other's point of view and to evolve workable methods and solutions. To that extent, CSA and RCSS have been successful in providing a useful forum.

# Post Conflict Sri Lanka: Nation Building Process

**2**

**Tissa Vitharana**

It is indeed a pleasure and honour for me to be able to address such a distinguished audience on, perhaps, the most important topic confronting Sri Lanka at the moment. We cannot dream of trying to overcome poverty and achieving meaningful economic and social development, without uniting our nation as one with a Sri Lankan identity and culture. We should look at our diversity as our strength. But, unfortunately this diversity has been used to our disadvantage by causing conflict situations to arise. In Sri Lanka, there are differences in race, religion and caste and these are exploited at various times to varying degrees. The focus today is on conflict, based on race which took the form of on an internal war, undertaken and led by the LTTE, as a separatist movement using terrorist tactics. This has been a major turning point in Sri Lanka's history. Another factor to be considered is that we have had Sinhalese youth rebellions, mainly in the South of the country in 1971, 1988 and 1989. These rebellions had their roots in having an educated youth who had benefited from the free education system of Sri Lanka, with many ambitions which could not be realised due to poverty and underdevelopment. The conflict in Tamil North also had similar root causes. But overall, we know that there has been a national question which has not been resolved. It is to what extent that we resolve this, to the satisfaction of all stakeholders that we would be able to find lasting peace in our country and work towards realising our potential as a nation.

The post-conflict situation, I think, has had its advantages and disadvantages. There has been significant progress in the area of rehabilitation, in restoring the displaced people to their origins. But in other areas, there are still shortfalls. I am not going to deal with them because I think all of you are familiar with the situation. But what is really at the core of reaching a solution to our problem is the forging of a political solution to the national question. The fact is that, during the war and thereafter for some time, the President supported the All Party Conference and the All Party Representatives Committee (APRC) process.[1] APRC went on for more than three years and had 126 meetings and came up with a consensus among the thirteen party representatives on twenty one political issues that required agreement. These were presented to the President and other leading members of the SLFP. Five of them were incorporated to varying extents with some modifications in the President's second political manifesto. Other issues still remained unresolved and the President has given an undertaking that the APRC process would continue, but that has not materialised.

But the President has set other processes in motion. One is the dialogue which started at the beginning of 2011, between the delegation representing the Government and the representatives from the Tamil National Alliance, which unites the several Tamil political parties in the Parliament (the main representatives therein of the Tamil voters of the North and the East). This dialogue has been going on and there are various reports. So far, one could say that it has not matured into something that would significantly take the process forward. In this context, an idea has been mooted to set up a Select Committee of Parliament to which all the parties represented in Parliament would send at least one representative, up to a maximum of thirty one members. When this idea came up within the Government, some were very keen to set a defined time period. A six month period was agreed on which can be extended, provided there is a failure to reach a consensus within that period. In my speeches in Parliament and outside, I have indicated that once the Select Committee meets and different political issues are identified or discussed, the starting point for the discussions should be, whenever possible, the consensus that was reached during the APRC process. After all, the consensus has been reached after fairly in-depth detailed discussions, taking our own reality into consideration. Therefore, if we make that the starting

---

[1] Mr Tissa Vitarana chaired the All Party Representatives Committee (APRC) process.

point for the discussions in the Select Committee process, it should shorten the time required for discussion and would also probably require only minor amendments to reach a consensus.

Once this process gets under way, we have to accept that there are certain compromises that will be required. One of the facts that emerged through the APRC process was that the President, the SLFP and several other parties, which I would say represent a Sinhala Buddhist lobby, were insistent that we should work within a unitary framework. So the idea of a federal solution which the Tamil National Alliance has envisaged, I would say, is not on the cards. We have to work out a solution, keeping in mind the political reality i.e., majority of SLFP in the Parliament and President Rajapakse's government enjoys a two-third majority.

The local government elections which were held on 7th March and 23rd July 2011 brought out a few other realities to the fore. Support for the UPFA Governments has further increased mainly among the Sinhalese and to some extent among the Muslims and Tamils. However, in the local government elections in the Northern Province, the Tamil National Alliance clearly won. This negated the expectations of the Sinhala Buddhist lobby who believed that by solving the economic problems of the Tamils, particularly in the North and the East, the Tamils would support the Government. This emphasises the need for a political solution.

But seeking such a solution, we have to keep in mind that there are extreme opinions on both sides i.e., the Sinhala Buddhist and the Tamil separatist lobby (very active both within and outside the country), with pressures on both sides and to some extent, these pressures give rise to forces that act as "spoilers" with regard to the process of seeking a political solution. Also, I would say there are positive features and some of these forces may indirectly influence the government to move forward with a political solution.

Therefore, it is in this complex environment that the progress of the whole process will be determined. The fact is that, from the Tamil side there are some who do not recognise or like to recognise any positive contributions that the Government has made towards solving the problems of the Tamils and see and highlight only the negative side. This is also true of sections of the media, not only local but also international. As a result, they have supported and influenced the separatist forces in South India, especially in Tamil Nadu. There are pro-LTTE forces among the diaspora, not only in the West but Southeast Asia. They all have an impact on the rebuilding process, which I would say is a negative factor. We know that, for instance, a leading politician in Tamil Nadu came out with the idea of having an embargo on Sri Lanka to apply pressure. And so you find, there are a number of negative factors. Just to give you another example, there is the Transnational Government of Tamil Elam (TGTE). When I represented Sri Lanka for the ceremony on the formation of the new government in South Sudan, one of the problems that were brought to my prior notice was the fact that the TGTE had close links with the liberation movement in Southern Sudan and was to participate in ceremony. The Ministry of External Affairs, Sri Lanka with the help of the relevant High Commissions and Embassies, exerted maximum pressure with success to avoid a show down. The Sri Lankan government is hyper sensitive to such situations. The international outcry on human rights violations during the last phase of war has accentuated Sri Lankan sensitivity. Such allegations make the task much more difficult for people within the government, trying to get the government to move in the direction towards achieving a solution to the problem.

No war has taken place without violation of human rights. I think, by definition, war is a gross violation of human rights may be to varying degrees. The question here is whether it is a Government policy to violate human rights. There will always be individuals who will violate human rights. As Gen. Raghavan mentioned, I come from the Socialist party – the Lanka Sama Samaja Party – the oldest party in this country. From its inception, when the party led the struggle for independence from Britain, the idea was to unite all people - Sinhalese, Tamils, Muslims and it is this process that we have always sought to take forward. And we have our sympathisers, like the Communist Party, in the North and the East. Let me assure you that we were deeply concerned about the fate of the civilians during the entire war period and we were communicating with them frequently. And now if you look at the war itself, during almost the entire period of the war, there were no human rights violation allegations. In the Eastern theatre, all the violations were from the side of the LTTE. Now the question of human rights violations came up only during the last period of the war when the LTTE decided to use the civilian population as hostages, as a human shield and took them along with them when they were retreating. It was during that period that the real danger came.

Minister Mr Dew Gunasekera of the Communist Party and myself, we were very worried about the situation. We requested the President to call a meeting of the party leaders in the Government and at that meeting we raised the issue of civilian casualties. The top personnel from armed forces were called into the discussion and concerns were made known. According to them, the only way to reduce the number of casualties would be to minimise the use of long-range weapons and resort to the use of short-range small arms, but this would increase the casualties on the military side. The President directed the military leaders to stop using artillery and long-range weapons and only to use short-range weaponry. Now we were very happy with this outcome. It does not mean that there were no such incidents thereafter; civilians could have been affected in the cross fire. There could be bad eggs in any Army, who would abuse the power of the gun and such things do occur. The Government wanted to minimise civilian causalities and I for one, am convinced of this fact.

It is, therefore, very unfortunate that this hounding of the Sri Lankan Government on alleged human rights violation is going on. It is putting the Government on the defensive. I think it would have been better if the Government set up its own committee of respected/ competent personnel to inquire into these allegations. Lesson Learnt and Reconciliation Commission (LLRC) which has been a much broader mandate, is also expected to undertake this responsibility. In my view, LLRC may not be able to devote the necessary time and energy to this task. In this context, with pressure from the international community and diaspora building up (the LTTE propaganda film which has been aired by Channel Four), the Government is very defensive and this is not helping to take the reconciliation process forward.

The outcome we seek has been purely from the point of view of a political solution. For instance, the majority of the APRC team, including myself, was for a federal solution. But having studied the unitary framework system of Britain where the Northern Ireland problem has been solved by adequate devolution, the APRC was open to a unitary framework, through adequate devolution of power and power sharing as a political solution.

Now, that process has been jeopardised. There is a fear among the extremist Sinhala Buddhist lobby about the whole idea of devolving power, as in the context of the results of the local government elections held in the provincial councils, it would mean that the Tamil National Alliance would get power in the Northern provincial council. If they get power in the provincial council, there is a fear that extra devolved powers, together with the forces which are hostile to the Government there will be moved to renew the demands for separatism. So these are the types of reactions that have taken place. And in my view this is very unfortunate.

We must look at it objectively. Having defeated terrorism, the Sri Lanka Government is accused of human rights violations, which in my view, do not warrant such a degree of attention. In trying to seek a settlement for this problem, we have to work out a rational set of actions in a more friendly way, without this degree of hostility, so that there can be cooperation on reaping the benefits of defeating terrorism. This has been done successfully in Sri Lanka and admittedly the LTTE was perhaps one of the most feared terrorist organisations in the world. It has killed not only a Sri Lankan head of state but, also an Indian head of state. In such circumstances, the international community needs to be more constructive, more positive and supportive of efforts of the Sri Lankan Government in reconstruction and rebuilding the post conflict state.

I have proclaimed very clearly the view of the Left, that there has to be devolution of power. We have to have adequate power sharing at the Centre. There is a lobby against us, from within the Government, and from outside. But the fact that there are opposing views does not mean that a solution based on devolution cannot be achieved. It can be achieved if the necessary supporting atmosphere is generated both within and outside the country. As I said at the outset, we have to accept the political reality that President Mahinda Rajapakse is going to be President for a full term and may be, even for another term. Though there are differences within the SLFP, by and large, the party will go along with the President. So, we have to work out a solution which will be approved of by the President. If we are trying to work out a solution that he will not go along with, I think we are doomed to fail. And I appeal to all stakeholders and to the international community, to view our efforts to work out a political solution to the national question sympathetically, supportively and constructively.

# Managing Political Challenges

# Emerging Trends in Indian Regional Policies and Approach to Relations with Sri Lanka

**3**

G Parthasarathy

India's Foreign Policy in the contemporary world will be guided by a number of diverse considerations. Now described an "emerging power", the predominant focus of attention in India will remain on fashioning an environment, both external and internal, which will help the country to proceed on a path of around double digit economic growth, with economic growth being as inclusive as possible. In a diverse and pluralistic country like India, the very process of economic growth will inevitably generate social, ethnic, linguistic and sectarian tensions. While corruption and criminalisation of politics are presently straining its body politic, adversely affecting economic growth and evoking public criticism, there is, nevertheless, confidence that India has the strength and resilience to overcome these challenges. Terrorism sponsored by radical Wahhabi oriented Islamic groups, is going to remain a formidable diplomatic and security challenge. The American "War on Terror" has dispersed but not destroyed the terrorist threat emerging from India's western neighbourhood. Moreover, with its demand for energy resources rising rapidly, India will have to focus increasing attention on the Persian Gulf, where over two thirds of the world's resources of oil and gas are located and regional rivalries and sectarian tensions have been exacerbated, following the American invasion of Iraq.

Over the past two decades, India has become accustomed to the Union Government being made up of a coalition of national and regional political parties. Moreover, with economic liberalisation, State Chief Ministers now have substantial powers and opportunities to seek and obtain foreign investment and collaboration. While regional economic disparities have grown, a healthy tendency of backward States like Bihar seeking to emulate the growth rates of the economically dynamic States like Gujarat, Tamil Nadu and Andhra Pradesh, has also emerged. But there is no question that as federalism strengthens in India, the actions of individual State Chief Ministers will also influence the domain of foreign and security policies. The Union Government was unable to conclude a landmark river water sharing agreement with Bangladesh recently, because of reservations of the Chief Minister of West Bengal. In promoting border security with Myanmar, mechanisms have been devised wherein officials of the four border States- Arunachal Pradesh, Manipur, Nagaland and Mizoram- are regularly associated in discussions with Myanmar authorities. The Chief Minister of Tamil Nadu is regularly consulted on issues of concern in Tamil Nadu on relations with Sri Lanka.

India has made sustained efforts for economic integration, not only in South Asia, within SAARC, but also with the rapidly growing economies of East and Southeast Asia. Over the past two decades, India's "Look East" policies have enhanced its diplomatic profile in its eastern neighbourhood. As a full "Dialogue Partner of ASEAN" and as a member of the ASEAN Regional Forum (ARF), India has concluded a Free Trade Agreement (FTA) with the ASEAN grouping, after concluding bilateral FTAS with two ASEAN members- Thailand and Singapore. It is now a participant in the annual East Asia Summit, which currently includes the leaders of China, Japan, South Korea, Australia and New Zealand (with the US and Russia scheduled to join), apart from the Heads of ASEAN Governments. India's trade and investment ties with the countries of East and Southeast Asia are rapidly expanding. Comprehensive Economic Cooperation Agreements with Japan and South Korea have been inked. Within South Asia, the South Asian Free Trade Agreement SAFTA, though limited to trade in goods, is regarded as the first step towards establishing free trade in investments and services, with the goal of progressively moving towards establishing a Customs Union and Economic Union in South Asia. Supplementing the efforts at economic integration within SAARC are moves for economic cooperation in the Bay of Bengal. BIMSTEC, an economic grouping comprising Nepal, Bhutan, Bangladesh, India, Sri Lanka, Myanmar and Thailand, acts as a bridge between South and Southeast Asia.

While there has been a marked improvement in the climate of Sino-Indian relations in recent years, the relationship between India and China is still clouded by mistrust. While China views improved US-Indian relations with suspicion, India retains memories of close Sino-US cooperation detrimental to its interests, during the Nixon and Clinton Administrations. There is concern in India about what is perceived as China's policy of "containment" of India, marked by growing Chinese interest in maritime facilities in countries like Myanmar, Sri Lanka, Maldives and Pakistan. China's supply of weapons to the beleaguered regime of King Gyanendra at a time when the international community was endeavouring to assist in a process of democratic change in the Himalayan Kingdom and its continuing cooperation with Pakistan in nuclear and missile development, have only accentuated Indian misgivings. China's growing "assertiveness" in its territorial claims on the Indian border State of Arunachal Pradesh, its efforts to undermine India's efforts for regional influence by opposing India's participation in forums like the East Asia Summit and the Summit level Asia Europe Meetings (ASEM), its ambivalence on India's candidature for Permanent membership of the UN Security Council and its attempts at the Nuclear Suppliers Group (NSG) to torpedo efforts to end global nuclear sanctions on India, indicate that dealing with China is going to be  major challenge for India in the coming years.

Despite these differences and challenges, bilateral trade and economic relations between Beijing and New Delhi are booming and the two countries have embarked on a series of measures to enhance mutual confidence. Moreover, on multilateral issues, like Global Warming and in the Doha Round of the WTO, common and shared interests and perceptions have led China and India to cooperate with each other. The Indian response to Chinese policies of "containment" and "strategic encirclement" has been largely defensive. But, as India's economic and military potential grow and the country's "soft power" expands, India is dealing with Chinese policies, by adopting more pro-active measures in its relations with countries like Japan,

South Korea and Vietnam, by developing a larger footprint in its relations with ASEAN and a more imaginative economic engagement with Taiwan.

At the same time, there are significant constituencies for peace and cooperation in both India and China. There are efforts collectively by India, Russia and China to cooperate in the evolution of a stable, multipolar world order, in forums like BRICS and the G 20. Conscious efforts are being made, to not allow tensions, particularly along the Sino-Indian border, to escalate and to widen engagement between India and China bilaterally, regionally and globally. Common sense dictates that there is enough strategic space across Asia for India and China to cooperate and develop to their full potential. India has taken note of China's growing economic collaboration with Sri Lanka but is confident that given the close ties and geographical proximity between New Delhi and Colombo, the Sri Lankan Government has been and will be duly sensitive to Indian security concerns, as its economic cooperation with China expands.

India's ties with Sri Lanka will inevitably be strengthened on the basis of growing and mutually beneficial trade and economic relations. India views Sri Lanka as a country whose past performance and potential for rapid economic growth (it is even now growing at an impressive 7.5% annually) make Sri Lanka a reliable and long term partner for bilateral and regional economic cooperation and integration. India has been committed to extending credits amounting to around $1billion for the upgrading and expansion of rail links and infrastructure in Sri Lanka. Foreign Direct Investment by Indian Companies in Sri Lanka now exceeds $ 500 million and Sri Lanka is today India's largest trading partner in SAARC. India has agreed in principle to collaborate in the construction of a 500 MW power plant in Trincomalee. Tourist traffic has grown with 125000 Indian tourists (20% of the island's total tourist traffic) visiting Sri Lanka annually.

India has been deeply concerned about the welfare and well being of persons who were internally displaced during the ethnic conflict in the Northern and Eastern Provinces. New Delhi is committed to construct 50,000 houses for internally displaced Tamils. Considerable assistance has already been provided to displaced Tamils, through the provision of building materials and agricultural implements. It is India's hope that the vast majority of the displaced persons will be settled in their original habitations as soon as possible. An Indian Cultural Centre has been opened recently in Jaffna and India intends to increase the number of scholarships and technical assistance it provides to Sri Lanka. India is committed towards the restoration of the Kankesanthurai Port and has also pledged assistance to improving of the Palaly airfield.

Even as Sri Lanka faces international pressures on alleged excesses by its army during the concluding stages of the ethnic conflict, India has taken the position that aims to promote national reconciliation in the country. I personally believe that in the type of brutal civil war that Sri Lanka experienced, excesses by both sides are inevitable and that statesmanship is necessary to heal the wounds of the past and look towards a better future, as Nelson Mandela demonstrated in South Africa. It is for Sri Lankans – Tamils and Sinhalas alike, to decide how best this can be achieved. India does not wish to be prescriptive on how the ethnic issues can be resolved. The Northern Ireland political situation was addressed within the framework of what is a unitary State. There have been a number of innovative frameworks suggested to resolve the ethnic issue by eminent Sri Lankans like Mr. G.L. Peiris and Mr. Neelan Tiruchelvam. What has to be remembered is that there are no victors in a civil war and the tension and animosities can be ended only by evolving a political framework broadly acceptable to all sections of society.

Sri Lanka and India worked together to arrive at a framework for the South Asia Free Trade Agreement (SAFTA). It is necessary as the two countries seek to extend the existing bilateral Free Trade Agreement into a Comprehensive Economic Cooperation Agreement, similar to what India is negotiating with ASEAN and has with Japan and South Korea. SAFTA has now to be strengthened by the development of a South Asian Customs Union and ultimately with agreement on a South Asian Economic Union. Unfortunately, India has not been paying adequate attention to fashioning arrangements for economic integration in the Bay of Bengal basin through BIMSTEC. This has necessarily to be done and measures considered to integrate the fast growing and resource rich economy of Indonesia with its Bay Bengal neighbours. The ultimate aim should be for India and Sri Lanka to have an integrated approach to issues on economic integration and security in their Bay of Bengal neighbourhood.

The end of the ethnic conflict in Sri Lanka opens new vistas for enhancing bilateral and regional cooperation between India and Sri Lanka. All Indians earnestly hope that their Sri Lankan neighbours will successfully develop a harmonious, pluralistic society and fashion a political framework that fulfils the legitimate aspirations of the Tamils, while guaranteeing the unity and territorial integrity of the country.

# Political Challenges: A Sri Lankan Perspective

**4**

**Rajiva Wijesingha**

Undoubtedly the greatest challenge in Sri Lanka at present is restoration of trust. On the one hand, there is fear that a separatist agenda has not been abandoned and on the other, there is fear that unity will be enforced by subordination of minorities to a dominant centre. Connected with these are fears about demographic change and militarisation. Conversely, the other fears of the majority are, in fact, distinct from the fear of separatism. They relate to worries about domination by a minority through disproportionate influence on governance.

I will look first at the challenges represented by the latter issue, since they are the easiest to assuage. They spring from a high number of Tamils in positions of importance in government in the period leading up to and just beyond independence. This factor arose however simply because of the better educational facilities available in the North, as well as the commitment to education evinced by Northerners, in view of the paucity of other opportunities in the area. Overcoming any imbalance caused by this is easy, since it only requires ensuring that good facilities are available island wide and that students all over the country are committed to education that will develop good administrators as well as entrepreneurs. At the same time, it should be recognised that the earlier imbalance was based not on race but on geography and that there are minority areas with appalling education systems, just as there are many majority areas that have good facilities. Reforms in the education system must be based on equity on a national basis and the ideal outcome would be employment, relating to governance that ensures equitable representation of all communities.

In this context, the government must also note that there is a greater commitment to educational excellence on the part of minorities and this should not be held against them. The recent experience of the Post Graduate Institute of Management in marketing a Master's course for administrators is a case in point, given that applications poured in from the North and East, with very few from the rest of the country. The remedy for that is not to penalise the North and East, but to ensure that officials in other areas too understand the value of high level education and training. Incidentally, enormous superiority of the Northern and Eastern Province websites to those of other provinces makes clear the greater professionalism of personnel in these Provinces. The failure of government at all levels to take corrective action in the other Provinces is a fault that cannot be laid at the door of the Northern and Eastern Provinces.

In this regard, I should stress the relative failure on the part of majority community administrators to understand the need to broaden their horizons. Tamil speaking public servants, perhaps, because they necessarily understand the limitations of the language, they function most readily and strive, as a general principle, to become competent in the other languages used in Sri Lanka. This then leads to better and more productive relationships on the part of Tamil speaking public servants with international interlocutors, including aid donors. Conversely, Sinhalese speaking public servants are often content to remain functionally monolingual. This leads to resentment and is obviously unfair on the capable and can be best remedied by concerted efforts on the part of all public servants to improve their communication skills.

This element relates to the other concern on the part of the majority community, that there is an in-built bias amongst foreigners towards minorities. There is some element of truth in this, but it arises largely from perceptions of discrimination in the past. Unfortunately, it is true that there was discrimination and in particular, discrimination involving violence, (attacks on Tamils in the first six years of the Jayewardene government). Though, all that is in the past, the memory has been kept alive by the separatist movement over the years. But overcoming that negative impression cannot be done by further discrimination, instead it requires a much better communication strategy on the part of government and a strategy based on facts rather than arguments of bias.

I have long argued that the government has suffered badly from its incapacity to tell sensibly and accurately the story of the last few years. It is to my mind a very good story, but unfortunately – perhaps an inevitable consequence of democracy – the government concentrated more on telling a story that would translate into electoral success and did not concentrate enough on winning hearts and minds on a wider scale. That must change. To do so, it is necessary to develop communication skills and work harder at understanding reasons for resentment and the perpetuation of a discourse, including in the international community that dwells on the deprivation suffered by minorities.

I have no doubt, such understanding with a commitment to remedial measures when there are good reasons for resentment, will do much to quell any residual urges for separation. It is minimal amongst minorities within Sri Lanka and measures that strengthen their commitment to a united country will soon dispel the influence of those elements in the diaspora that are still recalcitrant. They are not significant, but little effort has been made thus far to channelise the energies of those members of the diaspora who are peace-loving by nature into working together with the government, to improve the situation of the minority in Sri Lanka. It requires careful and concentrated efforts and the failure of the government to concentrate on efforts to convey to the diaspora, the positive measures taken and to involve them in plans for more, is regrettable and will contribute to further difficulties unless corrective action is taken soon.

I mention the need to involve the minorities in plans for more positive action in the areas in which they dwell, because one of the main reasons for suspicion and fear is that they are left out of planning and hence deprived of benefits that should accrue to them. I believe the enormous amount of resources ploughed in by the government to the North and East is ample evidence that the area is being developed in a way that never occurred before and which will do much to reduce the disparities that led to so much resentment in the first place. But the government has not taken special care to ensure participation of the targeted communities in planning and has seemed to adopt a paternalistic rather than a participatory approach.

This is not the whole story, for much has been contributed by senior administrators in the areas targeted. But because of a lack of communication between decision makers and the community at large, the impression that persists is negative. This is particularly the case in the Jaffna peninsula, where existing levels of sophistication demand greater consultation. While it could be argued that, in the Wanni, needs were obvious, and it was important to get the job done swiftly, the failure to ensure more involvement of all stakeholders in the very north has led to resentment. This was apparent in the comparatively low poll government received in many parts of the Jaffna District, as compared to the much better performance in a majority of areas in the Wanni.

But, even in the Wanni there is need to make clear that future development will be led by people of the area. This requires more concerted efforts at Human Resource and Capacity Development than have been thus far seen. Training at higher levels, encouragement of entrepreneurship, facilitation of micro-credit, support for cooperative community activity, recruitment of teachers from the area, involvement in security services, all these would help to increase confidence in the government and its intentions.

In the absence of such initiatives, distrust grows. This is accentuated by the continuing military presence in the North. Given the possibility of renewed efforts to promote terrorism, in particular, given the intransigence of former terrorist financiers and supporters in the West who seem to have the ear of at least some opinion makers, government cannot scale down to negligible levels, the military presence. It should also be noted that the failure of critical voices to appreciate the refusal of government to scale up that presence, as advocated by the former army commander, has contributed to suspicions that those voices are not genuine and are more anxious to denigrate the government than to ensure the welfare of the people of the North.

Therefore, the Government's concerns about deliberate lack of understanding of the pressures that had to be overcome to ensure swift resettlement of the displaced without the establishment of large cantonments as had been advocated are understandable. But it is also important for the government to understand the concerns of those who live in the area and act expeditiously to avoid any developing sense of alienation. It would make sense therefore to move swiftly to recruit more minority representatives into the security forces, not only the police – where what has been done already is not well enough known – but also the army and the other services. It is disappointing, for instance, that the Education Ministry seems to have put a stop to the heartening initiative of the Secretary of Defence to commission Tamil officers into the Cadet Corps through a program of training English teachers. This would solve two problems simultaneously, but sadly several government departments cannot think outside the box and develop initiatives that will fulfil basic needs and also contribute to overcoming political challenges.

Other areas in which the military could contribute actively to overcoming any sense of alienation is through training courses on the lines of the successful programme provided to students at university level. Though there were objections from politicians in the south, the target groups as well as other stakeholders have expressed appreciation of what was offered and achieved. There is no reason not to offer similar courses, not only for ex-combatants but also for youngsters who may not be qualified for government employment, given the decimation of the education system which the LTTE indulged. The Government continued to finance and administer schools during the years when LTTE controlled the area and continued with child conscription as well as military training in schools.

In a practical way, such training could offer basic qualifications involving languages plus vocational and aesthetic training, with a package that would allow those who were interested to obtain the six passes at Ordinary Level that would qualify them to join various branches of government service. A more streamlined approach to catch up education can easily be devised, which would also ensure the psycho-social attention, including through cultural activities and sports that many in the region may require.

I have dwelt at some length on training which may seem at odds with my subject - political challenges. However, I believe that the political problems that arose in the first decades after independence, before terrorism took over, were from discrimination with regard to language and employment and it is therefore vital to ensure corrective action that will prevent recurrence of either discrimination or of perceptions of such. In this regard, we need also to keep in mind the destructive impact of the monolingualism in which our youngsters were straitjacketed by the enforcement of mother tongue education on the basis of three different types of schools, for Sinhalese, Tamils and Muslims.

Sri Lanka distorted the right to be educated in one's mother tongue into a compulsion without any alternatives. Obviously forcing people to study in an alien language is counter-productive, but it is equally counter-productive to stop those who aim at bilingualism having opportunities to pursue this within the school system. It is also unfair to restrict choice in a context when it is the poor and rural schools that suffer, whilst the privileged have continued to enjoy access to English, which has then enabled them to enjoy employment at levels to which those stuck in knowledge of only one language cannot aspire. Our failure to learn lessons from the manner in which India and Malaysia have developed sophisticated education systems is culpable, but it is not too late for changes now.

Therefore, my argument is to think laterally to overcome challenges with regard to distrust and fear – and indeed to develop lateral thinking in the coming generations, to prevent them from thinking in terms of old formulas and oppositional dogmas to solve any problems that might arise. However I should also pay some attention to more obvious political problems that have arisen, first with regard to what I mentioned earlier, namely questions of land and demographic change and secondly with regard to governance.

Questions related to land come up for two reasons, one the fear of military taking over large swathes of land and the second, the fear of settlers being brought into the Wanni from outside. With regard to the former, it is sad that the government has not made clear its rejection of the proposals, which were put forth by some elements that involved a massive increase in numbers in the army, much of which would have been assigned to the North. As it is, the areas where the military will be stationed along with compensation that will be offered to those displaced should be clarified. The continuing reduction of the former High Security Zones makes it clear that initial suspicions are not valid, but the government has a duty to reach swift decisions on what is needed and provide equitable alternatives to those who lose their land. Continuing uncertainty about what might be planned contributes to corrosive suspicions which could be used by the unscrupulous, to exacerbate tensions.

These tensions are also connected with claims that Sinhalese who have no connection with the place are being settled in the Wanni. During my visit to the resettlement areas, I enquired about it and found this not to be the case. In all cases, it was clear that the families I had come across were driven away during the period of terrorist ascendancy and in many cases, they could lay claim to occupation for a century and more.

It is also necessary to dispose of the myth that the Wanni was a traditional homeland for Ceylon Tamils, who have been in Sri Lanka for centuries. On the contrary, a high proportion of those who were displaced were of Indian Tamil origin, as I realised while talking to them. Many of them could speak Sinhala because they hailed from the hill country. Some had settled in the Wanni in the sixties and seventies, preferring to stay back than to go to India under the Sirima-Shastri Pact, while others had sought refuge in the eighties, after the attacks on Tamils in the estate sector, which I fear Colombo took no notice of until Colombo itself was attacked in 1983.

I do not see this as colonisation or deliberate efforts at demographic change, as has been alleged, with regard to the resettlement programs, headed by Jon Westborg in the eighties, who later returned as Norwegian Ambassador to Sri Lanka at the time of ill fated Ceasefire Agreement.[1] Given the relative emptiness of the Wanni, settling Tamils were perfectly reasonable. We should, now ensure that they are given the capacity to exploit the rich resources of the area in a manner that contributes to national development as well as their own.

---

[1] For several years, Norway was involved in efforts to contribute to a peaceful solution to the conflict in Sri Lanka

There should be no racist comments of any sort about those who have gone back to reside in the areas from which they were driven by the Tigers, either southward in the eighties and nineties, as happened to Sinhalese and Muslims or eastward, to be used as human shields as happened to so many Tamils in 2008 and 2009. Careful explication of origins however, should be made available to assuage suspicions.

More importantly, this should also be done with regard to the fishing communities who are now able to return to their traditional migratory existence between North-East and South-West. However, the government should make sure that no alienation of land takes place as a consequence, while it should also ensure that fishermen from the north-east are also facilitated to migrate to other parts of the country at the required seasons. In particular, given the concerns about coastal development, information, in these respects, needs to be readily available. A mechanism to address any concerns would also be desirable, given the possibility that this is another area, in which negative feelings could be engendered.

Finally, I examine the question of political reforms. Though this is an area of greatest emotional stress, I should note that I believe it is only one aspect of a larger problem that needs to be addressed in different ways and in particular, through the social reforms and the enhanced communication, I have sketched out earlier in this paper.

Similarly, I believe that while talking of political reforms, we need to think outside the box and aim at satisfying not just the emotional needs of politicians but also the practical needs of people. In this regard I should note that the suggestions made by the TNA in discussions with government are a much better basis to proceed rather than the much more wide-ranging suggestions of previous negotiations.

Unfortunately, I cannot discuss those suggestions here, given the need for confidentiality. This is particularly important because there will be extremists on all sides who will pick on one or two aspects of a possibly contentious nature and raise tensions, instead of concentrating on the common factors that are far more numerous. I will therefore confine myself here to some general suggestions, based on principles the Liberal Party has been enunciating for years. In this regard, I should perhaps draw attention to the seminal role played by the Founder of the Liberal Party, Dr Chanaka Amaratunga, in formulating the policies which Mrs Bandaranaike advanced, while contesting the 1988 Presidential Election, as well as those put forward by Gamini Dissanayake and Mrs Srima Dissanayake who took over from him, as the UNP candidate at the 1994 Presidential Election. Unfortunately, in both cases, the policies were cast aside by those who exercised authority in the opposition after the Presidential Elections had been lost, though they have been referred to nostalgically, since then, on numerous occasions. I should also add however that these are my own ideas in accordance with development, since those elections.

Let me begin then by noting that the purpose of the government, as well as of devolution, is to serve the people. Reforms must target improvements in this regard.

The welfare of the people requires security, which includes financial security and food security and environmental security, in addition to protection from violence and crime. Security issues, as discussed, are primarily the responsibility of national governments. All areas in a country should however contribute to decision making with regard to security as well as other responsibilities of a central government. The best way of ensuring this is what most democracies have; a second chamber based on equal representation for all provinces or regions. Such a chamber should also engage in discussion and consensus building, which is not easy in the more combative atmosphere of the main legislature.

Many issues pertaining to the daily lives of people are best decided upon by units that are close to the people and readily accountable to them. In short, we need to pursue the principle of Subsidiarity, which sadly few political theorists in Sri Lanka advocate forcefully. Subsidiarity, I should perhaps add, is the idea that decisions must be made by the smallest possible units affected by such decisions. So individuals decide about their personal lives, communities about schools which cater to them and so on.

Many subjects in fact require close monitoring and quick responses that distant administrative units cannot provide. These are best administered therefore by small units. Reforms must strengthen the capacity of Pradeshiya Sabhas to deal with relevant issues, whilst ensuring that they are accountable to the people. Whilst necessary actions should be expedited, they must be in terms of consistent policy and with financial accountability to Provincial Councils. In addition, the allocation of resources is best done by a Provincial Administration, albeit with due consultation. Reforms must strengthen the capacity of such administrations to ensure appropriate structures whilst dealing effectively with problems.

It is also important to avoid duplication of personnel and efforts. Apart from being a waste of resources, this leads to limitations as to action, since responsibilities are not clear. Reforms should be directed to increasing efficiency. Streamlining personnel appointments and ensuring clear job descriptions is essential. For this purpose, the concurrent list should be reduced, to ensure clear cut responsibilities. Whilst many issues can be devolved, others will require central government involvement. Where concurrence is required, differences should be settled by consultation, rather than relying on the current catch all attribution of decision making power to the centre.

To sum up, the government should be exercised through :-

(a) A central government with a bicameral legislature that allows a greater voice to rural areas, through a second chamber based on equal representation for all provinces

(b) A provincial government with an executive that has decision making powers with regard to issues that do not pertain to security or national policy or inter-provincial issues

(c) A local government system that has administrative powers with regard to day to day issues, including social services and utilities

I believe discussion should proceed on the basis of principles such as the above, though of course these may require adjustment after all stakeholders have provided their inputs. A forum such as this should of course raise relevant issues, but as I have suggested, this should not be in terms of harking back to formulae developed under different circumstances. These principles I believe uphold the spirit of the 13th Amendment, while fine tuning it to add greater responsiveness to the people, greater responsibility to the various tiers of government and greater involvement at all levels of the people and their representatives.

# Political Challenges: A Tamil Perspective

5

**Kandiah Sarveswaran**

## Introduction

The un-witnessed war carried out by the Sri Lankan state to capture the North and Eastern provinces from the control of the LTTE is absolutely unparallel to any war of the post World War era. This war uprooted the entire population of the vast war zone area of the North and Eastern provinces with the support of almost carpet bombing from air and land. A variety of bombs were used to demolish the buildings/houses beside killing and maiming of civilians in large numbers.

This was a unique war on three accounts. First, it was absolutely unmindful of the destruction of civilian lives, their properties and livelihood. Secondly, the United Nations Organisation not only allowed the war but also neglected to prevent mass killing. Finally the international community supplied Sri Lanka with weapons, hi-tech surveillance facilities, and technical support and also gave a free hand to it to go ahead with the mission[1] which was contradictory to their approach towards East Pakistan, East Timor, Yugoslavia, Libya etc.

Constant bombing for almost three years displaced more than five hundred thousand people in the Northern and Eastern provinces. The bombing of men and materials continued till they were cornered in Batticaloa in the

[1] See for details UN expert report regarding war crimes. Also see the report submitted by Mannar Bishop Rayapu to the LLRC. Value of properties and amount of lives taken by this war is not estimated by the state. However almost entire livelihood and properties seems either destroyed and/or looted.

East and bottled up in a 3 square kilometre stretch of Mullivaikkal, in the North. The entire land mass was filled with armed forces who were empowered as de-facto rulers of these zones. Entire populations of Tamils in the war zone were uprooted and many hundreds became widows, orphans and disabled. Further, it was believed that many hundreds died subsequent to the war, due to lack of proper treatment of war wounds.[2] Defeat of the armed resistance of Tamils and the subsequent occupation of their entire traditional homeland by the Sinhalese armed forces[3], in large numbers[4], under the pretension of preventing any resurgence of LTTE, presented a de-facto military rule in Tamil provinces. The armed forces made their way into the personal/private, social, political and cultural life of the people and controlled the civil administration of these provinces.

The political history from late colonial era shows that the Sinhalese rejected the rights of Tamils and made every effort to establish their supremacy over the Tamils, and Tamils constantly resisted such efforts and asserted their rights. The Mahavamsa based ideology of Anagarikatharmapala that is 'Sinhalese are the sons of the soil' and the 'island belongs to Buddhist' seem to be the rationale for the antagonising relationship between the two communities. His preaching dubs Tamils and Muslims along with colonialist as aliens. The buses belonging to Sinhalese, running on Jaffna route have massive stickers with the slogan of 'this is Buddha's kingdom' pasted on it, slogans like 'let the Buddhism spread everywhere' is written on the new arch built across the A9 road in Kilinochchi (an almost hundred percent Hindu town). In reality, Tamils are exclusive historical inhabitants of the North and Eastern provinces are exclusive historical inhabitants of Tamils. Thus, these provinces were always treated as Tamil states.[5] Vast majority of the Sinhalese do not have any idea about

---

[2] Sri Lankan government refused to release the list of names and details of the people and suspected LTTE members surrendered during the war and kept in barbed wired camps and unknown detention camps. Still thousands of people are in dark about the existence of their kiths and kin.

[3] Even though armed forces of the island used to referred as Sri Lankan armed forces, in real sense it is almost cent percent Sinhala forces.

[4] Independent sources estimate that the proportion between armed forces and Tamil people in the Jaffna peninsula is 1:9 and in Vanni, it is 1:4 while the government claims that it is 30,000 in the entire Northern Province.

[5] From 1956 to 1983, in all the anti -Tamil carnages, Tamils were taken to Jaffna and eastern province by ships (not by train or road transport) for safety and protection.

the terrain, the people, and their historical, social, political and cultural roots and the ideology of the North and East Provinces. The majoritarian rule built up over the Sinhalese chauvinism neglected the history of Tamils.

Soon after the defeat of the LTTE, then Army General Sarath Fonseka released an open statement, "This is Sinhala Buddhist state. Tamils should not expect any special treatment as minorities. They have to accept this reality and live accordingly".[6] The statement of the current Army General, Jagat Jayasuriya, "..........all the army camps[7] the North and East will be made permanent; houses and agricultural land will be allocated to army camps." Linking this to the budget 2010 allocation of LKR, 1, 00,000 for every third child of armed forces explains the agenda of the state to convert the North and East Provinces as colonies of Sinhala Armed Forces

The magnitude of the cruelty of the war created a variety of humanitarian issues which displaced many Tamils. But the intentions of the state and the armed forces seem to maintain this status quo by refusing to resettle them in their own lands, refusing housing for them, depriving them from livelihood, abandoning a large number of the disabled and people suffering from a variety of chronic illnesses and by being insensitive about the education of children of these families etc.

## Pre-war Scenario

The post-war political challenges implicate a need for comparison with pre-war challenges. Likewise, post war Tamil perspective calls for a comparison with post war Sinhalese perspective because the Tamil nationalism emerged and grew, rather in response to the Sinhalese bigotry.

The struggle to reestablish the historical-political authority of Tamils in Sri Lanka against anti-Tamil racist[8] campaign of the state is almost a century

---

[6] Almost all the news papers published this statement in Colombo and Jaffna.

[7] Open statement given on more than one occasion, published in news papers.

[8] Angarika Dharmapala, father of Sinhala-Buddhist revivalism preached Tamils as Dravidians and Sinhalese as Aryan descents. This unscientific mythical thought was taken by the successive Sinhala polity to construct Sinhala identity and Sinhala nationalism. J.R. Jeyawardena, after the 1983 anti-Tamil carnage to emphasise this mythical identity, said his nose is as big as Indira Gandhi's and that proves that they are both Aryans.)

old. Scholars inaptly refer to this nationalist conflict as an ethnic conflict. Tamil nationalist struggle took different forms and goals in response to the aggravation of anti-Tamil measures of the Sinhala majoritarian state. The struggle began with the demand of communal based parity of representation and sparks of communal speech in an election campaign of Sir Marcos Fernando against Sir Pon Ramanathan in 1910.[9] Crossing many stages, the struggle at present is witnessing aggressive implementation of projects, aiming to complete the process of establishing Sinhala Buddhist supremacy to wipe out the identity of Tamils as a nation by occupying their traditional homeland.

From pre independence years, the Tamils tried to reestablish their due political authority as co-possessors of the island but the Sinhalese polity opposed it. Over a period of seven decades, Tamils demanded various systemic changes to regain their due rights in response to the changing attitude of the state. The demand to living together under a unitary state, with the constitutional assurance based on the principle of 'non-domination' in the form of 50:50 in legislative membership and in the government, was rejected both by the Sinhalese polity and the colonial government in mid 1940s.

The agenda of the Sinhalese polity to establish the island as a Pan Sinhalese Buddhist state was demonstrated by series of issues such as J.R. Jayewardene's Bill of Sinhalese as the official language in 1944 in the state council, 1947-48 twin Bills to ban citizenship for over a million Plantation Tamils and the enduring trend of government sponsored Sinhalese colonisation in Tamil Districts led by D.S. Senanayake, under the guise of agricultural development. This hegemonic attitude of the Sinhalese polity impelled the Tamils to establish political power in their traditional homeland i.e. merged North-Eastern provinces, to protect their land and to ensure their right to have political, economic and cultural life against assimilation designs of the Sinhalese polity.

Quarter century long democratic efforts to establish a federal system/ autonomy in North and East provinces ended with bitter experiences or

──────────────────

[9] See Murugar Gunasingam, *Sri Lankan Tamil Nationalism: A Study of its Origin,* (Sydney, MV Publications:1999)

rather implementation of multi-pronged suppressive measures to weaken the claim. Successive ruling regimes of independent Sri Lanka demonstrated 'too late too little' attitude and 'unilateral disownment of even the agreed too little powers'.

Lands were carved out of Tamil provinces and annexed to bordering Sinhalese districts to reduce Tamils as minorities in their own constituencies and shrinking their territory. Introduction of once redundant Official Language Act intended at assimilation through weakening of the core of Tamil culture and identity and revoking of minority safeguard from Soulbury Constitution, defied even the meagre space for justice to protect minority rights and made Tamils, political orphans.

Introduction of Buddhism as state religion emerged as another powerful tool to conquer Tamil lands. Introduction of standardisation cut down the opportunities for Tamils at higher education and in all kind of jobs. High intensity anti-Tamil violence was unleashed at regular intervals, pushing them into cycles of displacement, loss of lives, property and livelihood. Regular use of 'state terrorism' to suppress democratic protests by Tamils against the said laws and practices compelled the Tamil leadership to lose faith in democratic means.

Paradoxically, the pioneer of the campaign for federal system was S.W.R.D. Bandaranaike. He began advocating this since 1925, based on a two nation theory. Citizens of Kandy for more than a decade until the independence, advocated for three federal units including a federal unit consisting of North and Eastern provinces. The Ceylon Communist Party and its trade union passed a resolution recommending autonomy to the Tamil region i.e. North and East, based on the right to self-determination, if necessary, a secession which was sent to the Ceylon National Congress to be incorporated into the proposed constitution of the independent Ceylon.[10] In the recent history, Parliamentary Select Committee (PSC) under the presidency of Premadasa, accepted a federal system with divided North and East,[11] Chandrika Bandaranaike's political package too talked about

---

[10] See for details, Sarveswaran Kandiah, The Tamil United Liberation Front: Rise and Decline of a Moderate ethnic Party of Sri Lanka, Unpublished thesis.

[11] See for details, Mangala Munasinghe proposals 1993.

the federal system with re-demarcation of the boundary of the East[12] and finally an expert committee appointed by the President Mahinda Rajapaksa consisting of Sinhalese, Tamils and Muslims suggested a federal system with merged North and East provinces.[13]

They advocated a federal system as they realised that power sharing is essential in multi-ethnic societies to live together as one state with equality, solidarity and harmony. The question is why then, when ever efforts for minimal power sharing are made, do the dominant Sinhalese polities continue propaganda among their constituencies on the basis that sharing power with the Tamils is a sellout of Sinhalese rights and power sharing would lead to separation? Why do governments disown even minimal power sharing agreements?

A reading of the dominant Sinhalese psyche throughout the post modern history from the formation of Ceylon National Congress gives an answer to the above questions. For Sinhalese, Sri Wickrama Rajasinghe is a hero because he resisted the colonialists; Dutugamunu is also a hero because he defeated a righteous Tamil King Elara of the Chola Kingdom.[14] It shows that in the dominant Sinhalese mind, colonialists and Tamils are placed alike. This was articulated by Anagarika Darmapala, the father of Sinhalese Buddhist revivalism, who said *"Tamils*, Cochins and Hambankarayas are employed in large numbers by the colonists *to the prejudice of the people of the island* – sons of the soil, who contributed the largest share".[15] Thus, the anti-Tamilism is one of the major components of the Sinhalese nationalism. For the dominant section of Sinhalese, Tamils were aliens as colonialists. This ironic[16]Historical, anthropological, archeological, epigraphic and linguistic studies of cross sections of scholars suggest that the Saiva-Tamil civilisation

---

[12] See for details, 'The Government Proposals for Constitutional Reform'.

[13] See for details, Expert Committee Report 2007.

[14] One of the stories of Mahavamsa.

[15] Kumari Jayawardena, seminar paper on "Nationalism, Revivalist movement and ethnic consciousness in Sri Lanka" Quoted in Reggi Sriwardena, *Lanka Guardian*, Vol.3, No.3, 15 August 1980, p.14.

[16] Historical, anthropological, archeological, epigraphic and linguistic studies of cross sections of scholars suggest that the Saiva-Tamil civilisation is the oldest civilisation of the island and with the introduction of Buddhism, a section of the island's society divided and evolved as Buddhist-Sinhala civilisation.

is the oldest civilisation of the island and with the introduction of Buddhism, a section of the island's society divided and evolved as Buddhist-Sinhala civilisation. belief of Sinhalese coupled with the fact that the numerical majority became the trump card of Sinhalese polity to win elections in competitive vote catching politics. This use of the anti-Tamil card in politics gained currency, in turn as the main ideology of the Sinhalese polity. Increasing reflections of this ideology in the governance was the fundamental cause for the conflict.

This century old conflict could be classified under four major stages. The period of 1910-1946 could be identified as struggle for constitutional reform against British colonial government to have political representation based on the principle of non-domination (by Sinhalese polity over the minority) and against the tendency of Sinhalese dominance over the minorities. This was countered by clandestine agreements by the D.S. Senanayake led group with the colonialists, to obtain territorial representation systems, to have Westminister system of government and gained power of the entire island in their hands, enabling to establish Sinhalese supremacy over the Tamils' homeland.

1947-1976 can be classified as a democratic struggle for the federal system within united Ceylon/Sri Lanka and the successful mobilisation of almost all Tamils under one united Tamil party, the Tamil United Front (TUF). The Sinhalese majoritarian state responded with violent suppression, using armed forces and goons and arrest of Federal party leaders and activists at almost every mass protest. The state unleashed three anti Tamil carnages with the blessings of respective governments and placed the republican constitution that paved way for smooth passage to establish Sinhalese-Buddhist supremacy and left Tamils as political-legal orphans thus, as secondary citizens.

Lord Soulbury who suggested transfer of power to the hands of the majority Sinhalese, following the anti-Tamil carnage of 1956, regretted his 'wrong trust on Sinhalese leadership'. Also, Prof. Sir Ivor Jennings, who drafted Soulbury Constitution, also regretted the drafting of the constitution, which made Tamils as subjects to the rule of Sinhalese without understanding the dubious face of D.S. Senanayake. Though it was too late, regrets and the causes for such regrets of these two people who played key role in laying foundation for the state building process, prove that the modern day Sri Lanka and its Constitution was built, based on the wrong report.

The politics in 1977-2009 was largely dominated by armed activities of the LTTE. The state focussed on the means of the struggle that forestalled the world to see the magnitude of causes of the struggle and the hidden Sinhalese supremacist agenda. Even though the struggle evoked the attention of the international community, hiding behind the international agenda of drive against terrorism, the state successfully wiped out the armed struggle. The defeat of armed struggle paved way for aggressive implementation of assimilation and annihilation projects of the state against Tamils, adopting illegal or/ legal means and employing subtle and overt coercive administrative approaches.

The ongoing struggle is the fourth stage. The Tamil National Alliance (TNA) took the flag of right to self-determination. Means of the struggle in this stage are political, diplomatic and legal. Primary facets of the struggle are political, legal and moral rights of the Tamil nation to attain a right to self-determination, based on the UN charter and international norms. Driving force of the struggle is undeniably historical, political, legal and moral authority of the Tamils as a nation and aborigines of the island.

This stage can be characterised domestically with the strongest President in the world[17] with clear Sinhalese supremacist ideology (two-third majority in parliament). Strong anti-Tamil racialist, political and administrative leadership are placed for the implementation of these policies and projects. Highly politicised armed forces are deployed in the North and East provinces, to ensure the smooth implementation of such policies and projects. Above all, continuous existence of Prevention of Terrorist Act (PTA) and ethnically politicised law enforcement force and the Judiciary [18] are in function to sharpen the teeth of racialism.

---

[17] The Sri Lankan President, constitutionally the strongest in any democracy in the world and with the 18th Amendment, even the available meagre space for democracy has been removed.

[18] This is an accepted fact that led to the 17th amendment to the Constitution to have independent police and Judiciary. This amendment was never implemented but instead, the present regime introduced the 18th amendment to make the 17th one void.

Internationally, absence of armed resistance is viewed as safe to establish and expand economic ties with the Sri Lankan state rather than extend their support to the Tamils to have substantial autonomy. In an era of interstate relations gaining importance, the question is whether the necessary efficacy of diplomatic struggle on the part of Tamil leadership could be achieved.

However, little and sluggish space in international laws and norms and in the UN are the opportunities available, to have optimism to forward the struggle towards positive end. Despite the primacy of interstate relations in the international relations, resolutions for the conflict in former Yugoslavia, Indonesia and Sudan give a ray of hope. It is in this milieu that Tamil moderate leadership shouldered the responsibility to face the challenges.

Following sections of this chapter, we shall try to map the new scenario of the conflict and to enlist and analyse the dimensions of political challenge.

## The War

New challenges could be classified broadly under two categories. Firstly, the question of possibilities for resolution to the Tamil nationalist issue, based on power sharing which is not on the agenda of the government; secondly, finding ways to meet the urgent humanitarian needs to the war victims which is neither desirable nor permissible to the ruling regime. In both the cases, the state seems to be maintaining double standards. At the domestic level, ruling regime leaders including the President and some top bureaucrats have come out with anti devolution statements. But in the practical sense, the Sri Lankan government has to portray a democratic face to the world that they are interested in a negotiated settlement. Thus, engaging in negotiations is a tactic of the ruling regime. Similarly, while neglecting the multi faceted urgent humanitarian needs of war victims', leaders of the ruling regime are giving out statistics which are far from the truth.

The cornerstone of the Tamil National struggle is to protect their 'traditional Tamil homeland' or 'historical inhabitants' of contiguous landmass of North and Eastern provinces. Protection or securing of the territory of a nation in any multiethnic and multicultural state is a necessity to protect the identity of that nation, because culture, thoughts, literatures, lifestyle and all spheres of social and economic life of any society arises from the land which people of those nations binds with. In an era of democracy, the ethnic, linguistic, cultural diversities gained appreciation, legitimacy and accommodation. This accommodation within the country is based on the theory of 'right to self determination' [19] or accommodation as a new nation, within the global setup, based on the same theory.[20] Political power over traditional homeland is paramount to protect Tamils, their unique social, economic and cultural life.

In the case of Sri Lanka, the TNA and the international community, including the UN Expert Panel Report on the war of Sri Lanka, suggested restoration of the life of the uprooted Tamils and the need of power sharing. Neglecting these potential preconditions for any meaningful developmental, the state introduced two major schemes-the 'spring of the north' and the 'dawn of the east' which are clearly designed in establishing supremacy of the Sinhalese over the political, economic and cultural life of the Tamils. Armed forces play a major role in executing these tasks. More than the contradicting claims of the quantity of the forces in the north and east, tasks entrusted to the forces in these provinces pose the foremost political, economic, cultural and humanitarian challenges. While the government says that only 30000 armed forces are placed in the north, independent sources estimate the proportion of the forces and civilians in Jaffna to about 1:9 and in Wanni, this is about 1:4. Considering the numbers and sizes of the army camps and the amount of the visibility of sizes of the army, the latter could be closer to the truth.

## Issues of Power sharing

Power sharing involves issues of will of the state and the bargaining power of the Tamil leadership. The state mainly gets involved in its hasty multi-pronged land occupation spree, which is the core of almost all issues concerning Tamils. Armed forces are the key players of implantation of the policy of occupying Tamil lands. The land occupation has multidimensional

---

[19] Accommodative solution in South Africa and Federal systems in many countries.

[20] Yugoslavia divided as five states, East Timor emerged as a sovereign state out of Indonesia, Georgia asserted its right to self determination and very recently, South Sudan established its sovereignty through a referendum conducted by the UN.

impact on demography, culture, control of political power, control over economic development and the safety and security of the Tamils. Without these issues, there can be no meaningful negotiation. The solution also involves the issue of demilitarisation i.e. restoration of civil administrations in the two provinces.

During the conflict, all the governments wanted to go for a dialogue with LTTE. While in practice, the then governments denied to devolve powers such as land and police which were part of the 13th Amendment of the Constitution but gradually revoked even little powers devolved to the provinces, dealing with other subjects. The central governments used to utter verbal acceptance to consider power sharing, based on internal self determination in order to bring down the Tamil leadership from their demand of solution based on external self determination.[21] Considering the history of negotiations[22], the attitude of the state[23] and the ideology of the Sinhala polity, not only the leadership of Tamils but the Tamil people as a whole have a clear understanding that there cannot be any acceptable and sustainable solution, under the rule of the Sinhala polity. From 1983, all the negotiations held were due to the external compulsions. Both India and Norway were provoked and undermined to stop their role, by the GOSL, mainly to avoid possible federal solution that was advocated by these countries.

Subsequent to the defeat of the armed resistance of the LTTE, there were a number of statements from cross sections of the leaders of the government and state apparatus, in different tones, warning Tamils against asserting for power sharing. Reportedly, some ministers and MPs said that with the burial of terrorism in Mullivaikkal, the ethnic conflict is also buried. Soon after the victory the then Army General, Sarath Fonseka said that 'Tamils should not expect any special powers or privileges as minorities, as this is a Sinhala Buddhist state and they have to reconcile with this reality'.

---

[21] Eric Sole Heim, the facilitator between the LTTE and the SLG said that both the SLG and the LTTE were not ready to accept the federal solution.

[22] All the agreements aimed at solution to the conflict were done due to various compulsions created by Tamil leadership by themselves or with the support of external forces and never from the realisation to build a harmonious society, by any government.

[23] All agreements signed between the SLG and the Tamil leadership, including India-Sri Lanka agreement for resolution to the conflict were unilaterally disowned by the SLG.

A recent statement of the Defence Secretary, Gotabaya Rajapakse was that there is "no need for power sharing, the available system is enough". Jathiks Hela Urumaya (JHU) and Patriotic National Movement[24] have constant and vigorous stance against devolution. For instance, the 24 September 2011 statement of Patriotic National Movement warned the government that it would end up with the Libyan situation if power was devolved to Tamils. And finally, the President repeatedly said that he would not devolve police and land power to the provinces. The open denial of implementation of these subjects amounts to violation of the Constitution. However, the President speaks and acts, having constitutional and legal impunity.

This is not merely the stance of the ruling alliance but also of the Sinhala polity as a whole, which is evident by the statement of the UNP (main opposition party) Secretary Tissa Attanayake "since LTTE is not a factor, there is no need for discussion on power sharing". This statement not only justifies the armed resistance of Tamils but reflects on the intention of the Sinhala polity as a whole, against power sharing.

All these statements prove beyond doubt that the dominant section of the Sinhala polity even at a time when the international community is exerting pressure on war crimes and substantial power sharing are against devolution. The government seems willing to accept the pains to prevent international enquiry on the charges levelled by the UN experts' report and the suggestion of the necessity for political solution than accept devolution of power.[25]

Continuing rigid attitude of the Sinhala polity is manifested by the government's negligence towards the request of the TNA.[26] What is implied

---

[24] Both are directly and indirectly part of the ruling alliance.

[25] Important suggestions of the UN expert panel report on Sri Lanka are: 1. International enquiry against war crimes and Human rights violations, 2. Political solution to the ethnic conflict.

[26] The Tamil National Alliance had 21 legislatures. They were completely neglected in the entire post-war policy making, projects and activities towards Tamils and regarding northern and eastern provinces. Till date they were not allowed to meet the IDPs in Vavunia camp. International opinion after the war emphasises the government to go for a sustainable solution and TNA's requests to incorporate them into the planning and implementation of the humanitarian schemes, soon after the Parliament election of 2010 were unheard.

by all the above mentioned statements is that they do not bother about the mandate of Tamils.[27]

After almost 20 months of the end of the war, the government began talks with the TNA only due to external pressure. Also the government, as usual, needed to project to the international community that it is engaged in a dialogue for solutions to reduce the heat of the charges of war crimes and accountability for killings. From January - December 2011, eighteen rounds of talks were held, without achieving solution to even a single matter concerning either on devolution or on urgent humanitarian issues. Only in the last two rounds of negotiation, matters dealing with land power were taken up. TNA presented the rationale for devolution of land power but the government delegates did not have any justification to deny or change the reasoning of the TNA. However, they decided not to devolve it. Core issues of any meaningful power sharing involve land, safety and security of concern community and defined territory. In the negotiation history of Sri Lanka, devolution of land power has been accepted by all leaders from Bandaranaike to Chandrika. Land power was incorporated in the Bandaranaike-Chelvanayagam Pact of 1958 and also in the Government proposals for Constitutional Reform of 2000. The government delegation adopted an approach of 'beating around the bushes' and 'diversionary tactics on issues for negotiation' aimed at buying time in the negotiation process.[28] President Rajapaksa put an end to this futile exercise by declaring the government decision that Land and police powers will not be devolved.[29]

The victory of war boosted the Sinhala chauvinism to its peak. The state is engaged in militarisation and "Sinhala- Buddhisation" of all Tamil districts to demolish the Tamils' claim of homeland which is the very foundation of power sharing. It is clear that the project to change the

---

[27] In the post independence history of Sri Lanka no regimes respect the mandate of the Tamils. Hence, Democratic principles, norms and practices are either devoid or use as show peace for some vested interests in dealing with the Tamils issue. Tamil leadership was never consulted by any regime even when dealing with the matters connected to Tamils. It shows that either democratic values or reasoning of Tamils never heard rather only internal or external pressure some extent sensitises the Sinhala polity.

[28] Interview with K. Premachandran, Member of Parliament and TNA spokesperson participates in negotiation.

[29] President Rajapakse in the meeting with media heads in Colombo, 20.12.2011.

demography, deface the cultural outlook and capture the ownership of economic sources is to eradicate the ground of talk about power sharing. Thus, the space for power sharing solution to the Tamils is rapidly shrinking. The trend of the negotiation process seems leading to its logical end of proper implementation of UN Expert Report on Sri Lanka (UNEPRSL) under the guidance of UN.

## Humanitarian Issues and Challenges

Humanitarian issues largely involve:

(a) Forcible occupation[30] of private lands, houses and buildings of public utilities, particularly schools by armed forces or by Sinhalese under the protection of the armed forces;

(b) Deprivation of Tamils of North and Eastern Provinces from their livelihood;

(c) Concealing the details of entire detainees including alleged LTTE from public access.

After hearings of the complaints of the Tamils in its interim report submitted by the LLRC in 2010, one of the suggestions is to "*issue a clear statement of policy by the government that private lands would not be utilised for settlements by any government agency*".[31] However, according to the TNA statement, in response to Minister Mahinda Samarasinghe's speech in the UN Human Rights Council, on 12 September 2011,

(1) continuing displacement of near 200, 000 persons who have not been returned to their original places, who continue to be confined in transit camps or taken shelter with host families, including those displaced from Valikamam, Sampur in the East and several other areas in Vanni.

(2) The forcible occupation of agricultural and occupational lands

---

[30] Sampur in Trincomalee District, Kokachan Kulam in Vavunia District, Navatkuli inJ a f f n a Disrict, Madu in Mannar District and ...in Mullaitivu district are some examples of    em-bezzlement of villages.

[31] LLRC was appointed by the President in May 2010 and it has submitted the interim report on 13th September 2010.

belonging to the Tamil people by armed forces and persons of the majority community. No actions have been taken to remedy these blatant violations.[32]

Far from the truth, on 24 September 2011, in his speech in the General Assembly, the President said that 95 percent of the Wanni refugees had gone back to their home. The fact is that it is estimated by UN agency that 2, 60,000 houses were demolished and were to be built but at present, not even thousand houses have been completed.[33]

Some of the truths at the ground level given below are self-explanatory.

## Undeclared High Security Zones

According to the government figures, as on 1 July, 2011, 258,446 had been 'returned' or 'resettled' from welfare camps, leaving 12,661 in the Kadirgamar, Anandakumarasawmi (Zone 1), Arunachalam (Zone III) IDP camps[34]; only 7,440 persons remain in these camps, insinuating that all others have been returned or resettled.[35] What the statistics do not reveal is that over 2,00,000 persons in the North and East have not been returned to their places of origin. These persons either continue to be confined in transit camps or have been compelled to take shelter with host families. Such persons include those displaced from Valikamam North in the Jaffna Peninsula, Sampur in the Trincomalee District and several other areas in the Vanni. Moreover, several hundred families are unable to return to their homes, as large areas of land have been taken over by the military for camps and *ad hoc* 'High Security Zones' in Thirumurigandi, Shanthapuram and Indupuram, covering the districts of Mullaitivu and Killinochchi. These families have not yet been allowed to return to their homes and continue to live in camps without the most basic facilities.

---

[32] Quoted from the statement issued by the TNA on 14th September 2011.

[33] See TNA statement dated 14th September 2011, p.2, point 1.

[34] See Ministry of Resettlement, Situation Report as at 01-07-2011, at http://www.resettlementmin.gov.lk/ idps-_statistics.html.

[35] See Ministry of Resettlement, Situation Report as at 19-08-2011, at http://www.resettlementmin.gov.lk/ idps-_statistics.html.

## Mullaitivu

The 7,440 persons who remain in the Manik Farm camps are scheduled to be moved to Kombavil, in the Puthukudiyiruppu Divisional Secretariat, instead of their places of origin. Kombavil is a remote area in Mullaitivu that lacks infrastructure. The fact that it is located far from the sea affects the livelihoods of the relocated families, as the majority of these families are engaged in fishing. The government explained the reasons as the places of origin of these persons are either being utilised for business and military purposes or continuing de-mining activities in areas such as Puthumaththalan and Mullivaikkal.

## Amparai

In the Amparai district, Tamils are yet to be properly resettled in the villages of Thangavelayuthapuram and Kanchikudiyaru. Approximately, 150 families have voluntarily returned to these two villages and are living without any kind of housing, infrastructure development or other assistance. Schools and other buildings are still in a state of devastation and school children are forced to travel several miles to Thirukovil, which has resulted in school dropouts. Around 300 families are yet to be resettled in Kanagar Kiramam (Urani). Although the '30 houses scheme' intending to benefit the people of that area was originally planned, the military and the Special Task Force of the police continue to prevent these families from accessing the area. People from other areas have now begun to occupy these lands. Moreover, 300 families are yet to be resettled in Selvanayagapuram (Kottukal). These families were engaged in the cultivation of the highland agricultural areas and have been prevented from returning to their places of origin. 200 families are yet to be resettled in Rottai (Kilanguchenai), while a further 200 families have been prevented from returning to their places of origin in Thamaraikulam (Kaliiyapattai).

## Trincomalee

Seven thousand people were thrown out from five villages in Sampur area in the Trincomalee district. More than two thousand houses were demolished using bulldozers and buried without identity after the war. More than thousand school children were left in remote area camps and denied their education since 2006.

## Denial of Basic Amenities

Communities that have been returned or resettled, find themselves without basic facilities such as housing, sanitation, healthcare and education eg. Kokkilai in the Mullaitivu District and Krishnapuram and Vinayagapuram in the Killinochchi District. In the latter two villages, as many as 170 out of 658 families still live in temporary shelters.

The government has also failed to provide food rations to a significant portion of families in need of assistance. Conservative estimates reveal that at least 242 families are in need of assistance, as only 416 persons are currently employed amongst 658 families. However, only 128 families receive food rations. Hence at least 114 families who are in dire need of assistance do not receive any assistance. This is only a snapshot of the ground situation in the North and East, with respect to newly returned or resettled communities.

## Nature of Accessibility to Education and Health

The situation with regard to health and education in areas of return or resettlement is appalling. For example, medical officers are known to visit the two villages in Krishnapuram and Vinayagapuram, merely once every two weeks. This inadequacy has in fact resulted in avoidable deaths. Another matter of serious concern is the fact that the children of these villages are deprived of secondary education due to the lack of schools. Such deprivation is completely inconsistent with national standards and is a reflection of the socioeconomic discrimination faced by the people of the North and East.

## Nature of state Housing

In Vadamarachchi East, the Government commenced a 'resettlement program' just before the elections. Previous housing in the area was demolished and the stones obtained from the demolished houses were used in the reconstruction of the new houses. The new constructions were mere shells of houses, where walls were erected and painted, but no floors or any facilities were provided for, within the constructions. These houses were constructed in this manner for the purpose of providing pictorial evidence of resettlement, which would offer political mileage to election candidates. The constructions were far from a genuine effort to resettle people in the area.

## Militarisation and the Magnitude of its Impact on Tamil Provinces

Out of a total landmass of 25,332 sq. miles, Tamil people inhabited 7,289 sq miles of land in the North and East. However, after May 2009, the defence forces have occupied more than 2,702 sq miles of fertile and resourceful land, owned by Tamil people.[36] There is one member of the armed forces for approximately every ten civilians in the Jaffna Peninsula. The heavy presence of the military continues to be the most serious concern in the North and East. It has been more than two years since the conclusion of the war and the government has still failed to facilitate the proper transition of these areas from a situation of conflict to a 'normal' environment. The following sections of this report reveal that the high level of militarisation in the North is directly linked to other problems prevalent in the area. Such problems include:

1. State brutality including sexual assault;

2. Land grabs and occupation;

3. Problems relating to livelihoods of the people in the area;

4. The breakdown in the social fabric; and

5. Illegal intrusion into the role of the government, including administration and dispute settlement.

## Impunity

The prevailing culture of impunity within the military is a long-standing concern. When an incident is reported and allegations are made against the armed forces, state officials or private persons who are clearly acting under the direct or indirect acquiescence of state officials, no investigations are usually carried out. For example, there has been no progress on investigations into the attack in Alavetti as discussed below. Similarly, no progress has been made in investigations over the attack on the editor of the *Uthayan* newspaper, or the many attacks by '*grease yakas*' (*grease devils*) in the

---

[36] See Exclusive: Erasing the cultural leftover of Tamils to convert Sri Lanka into Sinhala country, August 24, 2011, at http://www.theweekendleader.com/Causes/615/Exclusive:-Inside-Lanka.html.

North and East, as discussed below. Moreover, no progress has been made regarding investigations into the assault on residents whose houses were burnt by an armed group almost a year ago.

## De-facto Judiciary service

The military is involved in the settlement of disputes with respect to land in the Northern and Eastern provinces. The Land Circular No. 2011/04 issued on 22 July 2011 establishes certain Committees of Inquiry responsible for resolving disputes regarding state land in the North and East. The committees include military personnel in their membership, such as the Area Civil Coordinating Officer and a representative of the relevant Security Commander. Military personnel are also appointed to an Observation Committee, which is established to assist the Committees of Inquiry.

The inclusion of military personnel in committees established to resolve land disputes is highly irregular and is illustrative of the deep and pervasive militarisation of the North and East of Sri Lanka. The Land Circular hence violates a range of constitutional provisions including Article 105, which provides that all courts, tribunals and institutions involved in the settlement of disputes, ought to be established by the Parliament. The Land Circular is merely an administrative circular issued by the Land Commissioner General. Moreover, this office has no apparent authority in law to issue such a circular.

## Snatching away economic life of Tamils

The military is increasingly involved in economic activity in the North and East. Through a system of checkpoints, the military ensures that its proxies control the transportation of fish from the Northern coastal areas. Large sections of beachfront land in the Eastern province have been parcelled out to companies that are headed by military officers. Moreover, the military has established a string of restaurants along the main Jaffna highway. The military establishment in fact runs an entire tourism operation catering to Southern visitors. The Navy uses state resources to run ferry services for the Southern tourist industry. Military personnel also run various quasi-commercial enterprises such as shops and salons, which impact negatively on the local economies. By appropriating the limited economic opportunities that might otherwise accrue to local residents to bring income and revenue to the fragile local communities, the military sustains and reinforces the cycle of poverty. With the access and advertising support of corporate entities in the South and the unfair benefits of highly subsidised cost structures through the use of state infrastructure, the military suppresses attempts at economic recovery in the North. In addition, the military has taken over several thousands of acres of land in Killinochchi, Mullaitivu and Vavuniya for cultivation without due process.

Army Commander Lieutenant General Jagath Jayasuriya is reported to have said that permanent Army formations in the North and East would be established with troops on duty, provided with permanent houses in those areas. He is reported to have said: "Army personnel arriving in those areas for duty are to be provided permanent houses and allowed to engage in cultivation work if they so desire."[37]

## Intrusion into Private life of Tamils

The level of control that the military wields over the private lives of the communities in the North and East is extremely disturbing. Families must inform the army of the guests they receive, their relationship and the reason and duration of their visit. Any family gathering to celebrate the birth or naming of a child, attainment of puberty of a girl, a wedding, or even a death, requires prior permission from the nearest police post. Every village has a 'Civilian Affairs Counter' managed by the armed forces where anyone entering a village is required to register himself or herself. Moreover, the army must even be informed of community activities such as sporting competitions. In a recent incident in Chavakachcheri, youth participating in a football match were brutally assaulted by the army, as they had played on a field without the permission of the army. Moreover, the military is heavily involved in aspects of primary education in Jaffna. The security forces in Jaffna even organised an award ceremony for students obtaining high marks for the Grade 5 scholarship examination. The Civilian Military Co-ordination in Jaffna, in its website, discusses the very active role it has in civilian life in the North.[38]

---

[37] See Army permanent in N-E, June 26, 2010, at http://www.dailymirror.lk/news/4656-army-permanent-in-n-e.html#comment-115184.

[38] See http://www.cimicjaffna.com/cimicnewsmenuMain.php. Also see appendix 1.

## Intrusion into Social life of Tamils

It is common to see the presence of soldiers in all civilian activities including village, temple or church meetings. Churches are required to inform the army of all meetings conducted for its members and a military representative is generally present at meetings as an observer. The military is also involved in deciding on beneficiary lists, in respect of housing and fishing licenses and takes part in all activities at the community level, including meetings to discuss local issues.

## Terror against Tamils – Grease Devil Phenomenon.

A series of attacks targeting women and which were sexual in nature have recently taken place in the North, the East and other areas of Sri Lanka. Such individuals have injured and murdered civilians and have commonly come to be known as *grease devils*, owing to their *modus operandi* of applying grease on their bodies to evade being apprehended. These attacks resulted in mass paranoia, fear and outrage in the North and East including in Jaffna, Puttalam, Mannar, Trincomalee, Batticaloa and Amparai. Public protests erupted in response to the widely believed involvement of the police and the armed forces in the *grease devil* phenomenon. Several incidents could be cited:

1. In Muttur, on August 13, 2011, a woman was attacked in her own kitchen. The attacker escaped but villagers followed him until he disappeared into a Navy camp;

2. In Batticaloa on August 17, 2011, a girl was attacked and her finger was cut off by an unknown man;

3. In Pottuvil, in August 2011, there were similar attacks on several women; and

4. There were complaints of similar attacks in Muttur and Kinniya.

Protests erupted over the refusal of the police and other authorities to apprehend these suspects. The protests were met with violent retaliation from the authorities, with the military and police arresting and detaining scores of individuals. Additionally, the police and military also carried out brutal, humiliating and degrading attacks against these people. The severe brutality with which these assaults were carried out has resulted in serious injuries and even in death. Individuals who were not even involved in the protests were arrested and assaulted.

## Election Related Violence and Intimidation

Election crimes that took place in Jaffna in the lead up to the 2011 local authority elections created fear among voters in the district. Both the Tamil National Alliance (TNA) and the Janatha Vimukthi Peramuna (JVP) complained that they were prevented from carrying out election related activities. Allegations relating to these election crimes were leveled against the government and civil armed forces. Some of the most blatant displays of intimidation were carried out against the TNA.

On June 16, 2011, in Alavetti, Jaffna, armed army personnel in full uniform attacked a local government election meeting where five TNA MPs were present. This was an internal party meeting that did not require police permission. In any event, both the army and police had already been informed of the meeting. Several security personnel of the MPs were also assaulted. Major General Walgama, who initially met the MPs soon after the incident, requested that the MPs refrain from lodging a complaint with the police. Moreover, the military official insisted that the MPs refrain from reporting the incident to the media. The MPs, however, did not agree to this and proceeded to make statements to the police. The incident was also reported to both Jaffna Security Forces Commander Major General Mahinda Hathurusinghe and the President. Major General Hathurusinghe initially issued a statement that this was a minor incident involving the army and the ministerial security personnel, but later claimed that he had been misquoted and assured the TNA MPs that if the army were responsible, he would take disciplinary action. No disciplinary action has been taken thus far, despite the MPs who were present at the meeting having repeatedly declared both publicly and to the relevant authorities that they are able to identify the perpetrators. On June 20, Defence Secretary Gotabhaya Rajapaksa confirmed in an interview to the Island newspaper, that in fact the army had stopped the meeting.

## Violent Suppression of Dissent

A 30-year-old male from Jaffna was found beaten and hanged at a playground in Achchuveali Thoappu in Valikaamam East, 12 miles northeast of Jaffna city. It was reported that the Sri Lanka Army intelligence operatives had harassed the victim two years ago. However, no suspects have been taken into custody thus far.

The shocking impunity of police act reflected in the brutal assault of an individual, which took place recently outside a courtroom in Jaffna. This individual was stripped half naked, dragged out and mercilessly assaulted in the presence of lawyers and public, while judges presided over proceedings nearby. The assault sparked protests by members of the Jaffna Bar.[39]

Other attacks carried out in the North by 'unidentified' groups are also a cause of serious concern. The most recent attacks include those against Thavapalan, the leader of the students union of the Jaffna University and Kuganathan, editor of the *Uthayan* newspaper. Thavapalan was recently involved in the mobilisation of students in democratic protests against the *grease devil* threat. The *Uthayan* newspaper is widely perceived to be critical of the state. Previously, a similar attack was carried out against the secretary of TNA MP, Suresh Premachandran on 27 April 2011. Thus, these attacks are widely seen as attempts to stifle dissent and freedom of expression in the North and East.

## Sexual Violence

The increasing number of sexual assaults carried out against women and girls in the Jaffna, Mullaitivu and Killinochchi districts, often by government officials and the military, is deeply distressing. There have been numerous reports of soldiers raping women. In most cases, victims and their families are ashamed and afraid to make complaints or file charges. The army also reportedly pressurises police to record that perpetrators are 'unknown' or 'unidentified' persons even though complainants have identified perpetrators and alleged the involvement of army personnel. Women and girls also face a serious threat due to the importation of Southern labourers for work on projects taking place in the North.

[39] See speech of M.A. Sumanthiran, M.P., Parliamentary Debates (Hansard) dated October 6, 2011.

## Continuing Harassment (ab)using LTTE Factor

Former LTTE cadres are threatened by the army to reveal the identity of those who supported the LTTE. In fear, these former cadres identify individuals with no links to the LTTE; merely to avoid further harassment by the army. The army thereafter begins to harass the newly identified family. Thus people in these communities have lost trust in each other. This has led to deep suspicion, paranoia and the destruction of close-knit relationships within the community.

## Conclusion

Sinhala polity is not ready to share power with Tamils mainly because power sharing would seriously hamper the implementation of the once hidden agenda, open at present that is to establish Sri Lanka as a pan-Sinhala Buddhist state. It was this understanding that led Chelvanayagam and the TULF in the famous Vaddukoddai resolution to declare the reestablishment of the once lost sovereignty to the colonialist as the only way out for the Tamils to live as a dignified nation. The Sinhala polity branded the TULF as terrorists. The then main opposition leader Amirthalingam was attacked by a policeman[40]; instead of taking action against the police, the Parliament took up a no confidence motion against him.

The armed resistance to carry forward the resolution of the moderate TULF was the direct response to the decades' long practice of state terrorism against democratic resistance and racist practices of the Sinhalese polity. In the struggle, the means were over-emphasised with the evil intention to suppress the ends by the state, the international community failed to articulate the refutation of the state to accommodate the Tamils for decades, which has the responsibility to address the issues of her people.

It was open direct violence employed by the state armed forces until the end of the war. Presence of Tamil armed resistance was able to prevent access to the large part of the Tamil's homeland obscured structural and cultural violence against Tamils. The war to 'liberate Tamils from the clout

---

[40] Main opposition leader, from 1977-1983, Amirthalingam was attacked by a police constable while questioning their atrocities in Jaffna in 1978.

of LTTE' resulted in aggressive structural violence, cultural violence and subtle form of direct violence against Tamil civilians.

The heavy presence of the military continues to be the most serious concern in the North and East for the effective implementation of structural and cultural violence against Tamils. The fact that despite the lapse of two years after the conclusion of the war, the government has failed to facilitate the proper transition of these areas from a situation of conflict to a 'normal' environment, could be seen as one evident for structural violence. Armed forces employ subtle way of direct violence at regular intervals against Tamils to maintain free passage for the implementation of such projects.

Dominant Sinhalese perception is that the Tamils are undue headache and not willing to accept either separation or substantial devolution. Tamils on other hand need their land and political power over the territory. The defeat of Tamil resistance created enormous challenges and some opportunities to both the communities. The question is how far these challenges can be met and the opportunities be utilised.

Rejecting the need for power sharing, continuing exertion of manifold harassment including denial of resettlement for uprooted Tamils in their own developed lands, as well as a land grabbing spree of the government under well planned and innovative means are the major challenges in the post war Sri Lanka. Equally, the settling of Sinhalese with the intention of changing the demography of the North and East provinces reduced the type of conflict from one of solution seeking to one related to the question of existence to extinction. The challenge is whether the Tamils will exist with autonomy, as a nation or reduce to the status of 'aboriginal Red Indians in USA' and perish.

The existence of Tamils with dignity as a nation, could be determined by the implementation of UNERSL. UN has to prove its integrity and protect its dignity by implementing the UNERSL report recommendations. Considering the ideology and practice of the Sinhala polity towards Tamils, the history of causes for negotiations and integrity of the state in the implementation of agreements and the vulnerability of the existence of Tamils as dignified entities, draws the attention of the International community to think about adopting paradigm shifts in the approach towards this conflict not only to protect Tamils but also to uphold international laws and norms.

# A National Perspective
# 6 Through Muslim Eyes

**Ambassador Javid Yusuf**

To gain an accurate understanding of the approach of Muslim community to rebuilding of society, it is necessary to first comprehend a Muslim's outlook to life itself. For Muslims, religion is the most important aspect in life and hence the approach to public affairs would be premised upon a system of values of Islam. Religion for Muslims is more than a mere system of beliefs and practices that govern their private lives. Rather, it is an ideology that embraces all spheres of human life and living, both public and private. In a nutshell, it is both a way of life and living.

Logically following on, politics and political issues then become important to Muslims to the extent that it facilitates the pursuit and practice of their religion. This is manifested in the somewhat pacifist role of Muslims that is evident in their political behaviour and the absence of political militancy in the national arena in post-independence Sri Lanka.

The developments since the end of the armed conflict in Sri Lanka in May 2009 are examined below, within such a contextual backdrop. The comprehensive defeat of the LTTE has provided an opportunity to address the task of nation building, unhindered by the preoccupation of a debilitating armed struggle, which has been a drain on national resources. The neutralisation of the LTTE has *ipso facto* created a vacuum that long dormant economic forces have moved in to fill. Even if the State did nothing on the economic front, I dare say that the economy will take off with the removal of the brakes on development that the armed conflict effected. However with the Sri Lankan Government's efforts to ensure large infrastructure development in the past two years, healthy growth rates have been achieved. That said, much remains to be done and the impressive economic achievements ought to be translated into meaningful and equitable benefits that will impact on the ordinary man's day to day life.

Recently I came across an Indian remarking that while India is doing well economically, it is not so for the Indian people. I do not know whether this is true or not of India. In Sri Lanka's case, however, it is closer to the truth because despite rapid infrastructure and other development, the less privileged sections of the citizenry face a significant struggle to make both ends meet.

However, the most challenging task at this point of time is undoubtedly the dealing with political issues that confront us in the post war context. Before addressing such issues, it is important to frame the discussion within accurate parametres and understand the context in which the conflict arose.

Many writers and thinkers, both in Sri Lanka and abroad have used the label 'ethnic conflict' to describe the events of the past three decades without clearly explaining what they mean by the phrase 'ethnic conflict'. This has led to considerable confusion and misunderstanding as to the nature of the conflict and consequently the possible solutions that could be examined. As a result of the conflict being loosely described as an ethnic one, many Sri Lanka watchers, particularly those living abroad, have come to believe that it arose due to the majority Sinhalese oppressing the minority Tamils and that the LTTE's armed struggle was to liberate the Tamil community from such oppression.

Such a perception in my view is in variance with reality. The Tamil community's campaign was against State structures and policies that were considered discriminatory of the Tamils rather than one against the Sinhala majority. The failure of the dominant sections of the Sinhala polity to address these grievances, the lack of a rigorous examination of policy formulation by governments of the day that would have identified possible adverse impacts on minorities (e.g. the Sinhala Only Act which elevated Sinhala to official language status without conferring a similar status to the Tamil language, standardisation of admissions to Universities which required Tamil medium students to obtain higher marks than their Sinhala counterparts), and the Tamil political leadership creating unrealistic expectations among the Tamil youth, contributed to the birth of Tamil militancy. Finally, the democratic Tamil political leadership lost control and the LTTE hijacked the Tamil struggle with disastrous consequences for both the Tamils as well as the country as a whole.

With the emergence of armed groups in support of Tamil demands, the entire conflict assumed a new complexion with attacks and counter attacks, resulting in the death of large number of civilians. With the LTTE often targeting innocent civilians, they earned the label of 'terrorists' thus blurring the distinction between the causes and the tactics and providing a handle for spoilers to dub it a 'terrorist problem'. Attitudes began to harden in certain sections of society on both sides of the communal divide, making it difficult for the moderates to advocate for a just solution through negotiations.

With the LTTE showing a great deal of intransigence at and around the negotiating table, the calls for a military response grew louder and stronger and it was an increasingly difficult task for those espousing a negotiated settlement, to obtain support from the long suffering public.

The Government of President Mahinda Rajapakse which took office in 2005, despite having in its ranks, hardline proponents of a military solution, traversed the path of previous Governments and attempted to negotiate with the LTTE. The LTTE repeated its mistakes of the past and failed to show any signs of seriousness in trying to realise Tamil aspirations through negotiations. When they made the tactical blunder of assassination attempts on the Defence Secretary, the Army Commander and finally shutting off the water supply used by the farmers of Mavil Aru in the Eastern Province to irrigate their fields, the Government was left with no other alternative than to embark on a military campaign to defeat the LTTE, which was completed in May 2009.

While the grievances of Tamils need to be addressed sooner than later, the pursuit of these goals by the LTTE, by resorting to arms was a strategic mistake. Armed struggle is an aberration and an attempt at a 'quick fix' of complex political problems that can, neither theoretically nor practically, result in a solution that is sustainable. Similarly, those against whom armed force has been directed are left with the feeling that solutions have been extracted from them through force of arms rather than the power of reasoning and hence are difficult to maintain. Placing all their eggs in the armed struggle basket has cost the Tamils dearly and left them without an alternative, when such a strategy failed.

The self-defeating nature of the LTTE's strategy and its military defeat has left Tamils worse off than they were, prior to embarking on an armed struggle. Their grievances remain and have in fact increased due to the consequences of the armed struggle with many of their kith and kin maimed or killed, their homes and livelihoods destroyed and faced with the daunting task of rebuilding their lives from next to nothing. Internally, Tamil society is brutalised, Tamil culture has been destroyed and the LTTE's intolerance of dissent and democracy has weakened the proud intellectual spirit of Tamil society.

Accordingly, in the post-war environment it is necessary then for the Tamil community to engage in serious introspection, with regard to their role and place in Sri Lanka and the strategies they need to adopt to ensure their rightful place in the rebuilding of the country. They have to learn lessons from the experiences of their past and reintegrate within the Sri Lankan society. Dissatisfaction with treatment meted out to the Tamil community by the Sri Lankan State should not motivate the former to the position of withdrawing from mainstream political activity that will, in the long run, prove to be detrimental to its own interests.

The Tamil community is an important and integral part of the Sri Lankan nation. However, in recent times, its preoccupation with the struggle to address the community grievances *vis a vis* the Sri Lankan State has resulted in them opting out of the national mainstream and not participating in discussions and activities, relating to matters affecting the country as a whole. While the Tamil political leadership will vigorously debate in the National Legislature, the importance of ensuring that Tamil regions secure its share of economic development, it will make little or if at all only a lukewarm contribution to the discussion on how to ensure the formulation of policies that affect the economic growth in the country. As such, it becomes imperative that the Tamil political leadership launch on a course of rethinking its actions of the past, coupled with clarifying its role in ensuring that the Tamil community is reintegrated into national life with dignity and honour.

While the Tamil National Alliance (TNA) could be excused for conceding the centre stage to the LTTE on account of its brutal nature and targeting of Tamil political leaders who did not toe the line, there was little justification for the TNA to be over-enthusiastic in espousing the LTTE cause during the years of the armed conflict. Such a strategy has dented the TNA's credibility and given Sinhala hardliners a handle to brand it 'LTTE proxies' whenever the latter seeks to scuttle solutions proposed by the former.

One advantage that the TNA has is that its leadership is, for the most part, untainted by any allegations of self serving opportunism or corruption and is recognised for not having forsaken its goals at any point to either the lure of political office or financial reward. This can be a constructive platform for it to build upon in making a public declaration that the armed struggle waged by the LTTE was a mistake, both from the Tamil point of view as well as from the national interest point of view. Although this may be asking too much from the TNA, if they can summon the political courage to do so it would eventually augur well for both the Tamil community's interests as well as the larger national cause. Such a public declaration will undoubtedly provide the TNA leadership, considerable moral strength, when canvassing for and advocating the rights and aspirations of the Tamil community in the political discourse of the country.

The addressing and resolution of political issues affecting the minorities is a crucial aspect of a strategy to achieve national reconciliation, leading to nation building. In this task, the Sri Lankan State ought to perform a critical, if not a lead role. It must be realised that although the majority of the Tamils did not support and approve the LTTE's resort to an armed struggle, the defeat of the LTTE and the fallout of the military campaign has left the Tamils a demoralised and wounded community.

The Muslims, on the other hand, are uncertain as to how any actions of the State in addressing Tamil grievances, will affect them. This has been the perennial dilemma facing the Muslims through the years when the LTTE waged war against the Sri Lankan State. The failure of large sections of the

Muslim political leadership, often characterised by opportunistic self interest rather than the needs of the community, further exacerbated this dilemma.

In contrast with the Tamil community which challenged State structures as a means of addressing its grievances, the Muslims strode a separate political path opting to engage with the State and work within the mainstream of Sri Lankan politics. This resulted in a great deal of misunderstanding among the Tamils of the Muslims strategy and caused a strain in relationships between the two communities.

The Muslim political leadership either failed or made no attempt to explain the reasons for the difference in strategy of the Muslim community in contrast to that adopted by the Tamils. Therefore, the former was unable to make the latter realise that such a strategy was adopted from a perspective of what was considered best for the Muslims and was in no way designed to deliberately undermine the Tamil struggle. The opportunism of Muslim political leaders from the conflict areas, forsaking Muslim community interests in return for Cabinet posts and other incentives, compounded the perception that the Muslim community was seeking to undermine the Tamil cause.

The Muslims, despite not being direct protagonists in the armed conflict between the LTTE and the Sri Lankan State, have undergone considerable suffering during the years of fighting in the North and East. The forcible eviction of the entire Muslim community from the Northern Province by the LTTE, the massacre of hundreds of Muslims who were engaged in worship in mosques in Kattankudy and Eravur, the taking over of lands belonging to the Muslims by the LTTE in the Eastern Province, the deprivation of the livelihoods of the Muslims in the conflict areas and the failure of the Sri Lankan State to provide adequate security to the Muslims are among the factors that contributed greatly to the sense of insecurity and unease that the Muslims faced as a result of the armed struggle waged by the LTTE.

Thus, as stated earlier in this chapter, the State ought to play the significant role and take pro active measures in order to rebuild society in the post LTTE period. The State must reach out and embrace the Tamil community, making them feel that they are as important a segment of Sri Lankan society as Sinhalese and Muslims. Such an effort must not be limited to smooth rhetoric but rather be combined with specific steps that make the Tamils feel that the Sri Lankan State sincerely cares and will ensure political, economic and social justice for all communities.

Moreover, in the post war context, it is paramount that the Sri Lankan State demonstrates by its actions that the Tamil community is trusted and shall enjoy a dignified existence in post-war Sri Lanka. Further, sensitivity to fears and apprehensions of the Tamil community, even if at times considered misplaced or exaggerated, becomes imperative to achieving the aforementioned. For instance, certain Tamil politicians have labelled the Sri Lankan Army a 'Sinhala Army of occupation.' This in this writer's view is a misguided description of the Sri Lankan State's official Army. That said, the concerns arising out of this misperception, must be taken into account in formulating post-war policy for the North and the East.

The Army's dominance of the higher levels of administration in the North and East as well as its intense visible presence at ground-level is not conducive to creating an environment of reintegration and reconciliation for the Tamil community with the rest of the country. If an assessment of the security situation leaves no option but the presence of the Army in the region, it must then recede to the background for the present and eventually work towards withdrawal from the region in a phased manner.

Moreover, it is critical that the State intervenes to dispel doubts and uncertainties of the Muslims with regard to the nature and content of a solution that may finally emerge. In the deliberations and negotiations that precede the crystallisation of such a solution, the State will be well advised to ensure that the Muslims are provided an opportunity to participate in and shape the outcome of talks. The issue of the forcibly evicted Muslims of the Northern Province and the livelihood and security issues of the Muslims of the Eastern Province must be central to any solution that is finally forged to resolve the issues which have cost the country and its people dearly.

Moreover, in its resolve to forge a solution, the Sri Lankan State must not lose sight of the need to allay the fears and anxieties of the Sinhalese people, who, despite being a majority have their own share of concerns, both real and imagined. Any solution that is meant to address the concerns of the Tamils and Muslims must not be at the expense of the Sinhalese. This will not only be fair and just but ensure the sustainability of the solution in the long run.

Finally, the three communities must work tirelessly to establish governance, administration and social structures that foster interdependence among themselves. This will help cultivate the feeling in each of the communities that the progress or downfall of each of them is inextricably linked with the progress or downfall of all other communities and the nation. This, in turn, will be invaluable in inculcating a strong sense of nationhood among the members of the different communities in Sri Lanka.

# Socio-Economic Challenges

# Socio-Economic Challenges of Post-Conflict Reconstruction in Sri Lanka[1]

**7**

**Saman Kelegama**

Sri Lanka is recovering from a 26 year separatist conflict, which significantly suppressed the livelihoods of people in conflict affected regions, damaged the natural environment, curbed the country's economic growth and incurred losses to many human lives.

Since the war ended in May 2009, Sri Lanka has experienced high growth amidst the backdrop of the global economic downturn. However, while the near term outlook promises higher growth, there are many challenges that the country will face as it rebuilds the conflict affected areas.

This chapter aims at taking a broad overview of a number of challenges. The issues taken up are: poverty reduction, education, employment and skills development, health, agricultural development, infrastructure development, expansion on tourism, industrial development and environmental and natural resource-based challenges. Some policy options are highlighted from an overall perspective.

## Poverty Reduction

The war in Sri Lanka was responsible for destroying infrastructure mainly in the conflict stricken areas. The entire road transport network and railway lines in the Northern and Eastern provinces were severely damaged. This

---

[1] Points collected, based on a power point presentation made at the Conference, organised by CSA & RCSS on 26 September 2011 and not an essay on the subject.

includes the A9 road which connected the Jaffna District and the southern parts of the country. As a result, these provinces were poorly connected to the rest of the country.

The war also negatively impacted the livelihoods of people living in conflict areas by the destruction of their assets, incurring losses, inflicting death on family members, destruction of financial markets and the reducing of accessibility to other parts of the country. These negative impacts were exacerbated by the key safety net program – Samurdhi Poverty Alleviation Scheme – not operating in some conflict affected areas before the liberation of those areas due to the collapse of the administrative structure.

In 2010, the Northern Province's share of GDP was 3.4 %. Per capita income stood at SLRs. 161K (US$ 1463), which was just 59 per cent of the national average of SLRs. 271K (US$ 2464) and the poverty rate was at least double that of the country as a whole.[2] Thus, an accelerated development has become a priority in these areas.

There have been initiatives by the government to reduce poverty levels and embark on socio-economic development in the North and East. *Negenahira Navodya* (2007) and *Uthuru Wasanthaya* (2009) were two such projects that have been carried out to reconstruct the damaged infrastructure and try to provide adequate electricity supply, roads, transport, water supply and sanitation, educational facilities, health facilities, employment, etc., for the people affected by the conflict.

The majority of the internally displaced persons (IDPs) have returned to their homes. The consequent challenge is to ensure that efforts are made to meet the entitlement losses that perpetuate poverty and to solve the social inequality, especially in the war affected areas.

Conflicts can generate poverty both directly and indirectly. Poverty is directly felt through the loss of public entitlements and indirectly through the loss of market/livelihood entitlements and loss of civil/social entitlements.[3]

---

[2] 'Investing in the Northern Province: Constraints and countering them', *The Island*, 28 Dec 2011

[3] *Sri Lanka: State of the Economy 2010*, Institute of Policy Studies of Sri Lanka, Colombo.

- Loss of public entitlements – e.g., closure of the A9 road, destruction of transportation systems and public infrastructure, including schools and hospitals.

- Loss of market entitlements – e.g., inaccessibility of fields/markets, disruption of normal trade patterns, reduced employment opportunities, depletion of resource endowments.

- Loss of civil entitlements – e.g., destruction of social capital (institutions, social networks), collapse of state-run service provision.

*Maga Neguma* (regional), *Gama Neguma* and *Gemidiriya* (village level) are projects carried out supplementary to *Negenahira Navodaya* and *Uthuru Wasanthaya* to develop the infrastructure. However, these programs suffer from a lack of funding and there needs to be more focus on allocating funds in proportion to prevailing levels of poverty and population in each village.

Market entitlements are being gradually met through *Gemidiriya,* which focusses on improving the intra-village connectivity and building grassroots ICT initiatives. However, emphasis should be given to linking villages to markets and urban centres, which is necessary for the agricultural sector.

In order to provide the civil entitlements in these areas, provisions of micro-credit and macro-insurance facilities need to be established, which are essential for coping with income shocks.

Increased investment in human capital is also needed to ensure that people take advantage of the new opportunities being created. This could help prevent inter-generational transmission of poverty.

## Education

The conflict has affected the education of the students in the war ravaged areas. Displacement, loss of family members, psychological impact, loss of school materials and destruction of school buildings and properties are some of the factors that led to disruption of formal and non-formal educational structures in these areas.

Education can contribute significantly to rebuilding shattered societies. Giving conflict-affected children a good education could be an integral part of social reconstruction, especially for the next generation. There are several issues that need to be considered in providing educational services for the conflict affected groups.

The war damaged educational infrastructure needs to be resuscitated. Essential materials such as furniture, teaching and learning aids should be provided to students to make school life attractive, once again.

Dealing with ex-child combatants will be a challenge that needs careful handling. Necessary steps should be taken to help these children who need psycho-social support. Furthermore, as most of the children in these areas would need help in dealing with the psychological impacts the war has caused them, schools could be a place where such matters were dealt with.

Adequate human and financial resources should be provided to these areas to ensure that these children are given a good education. Not only should the teachers teach the subject requirements, but also incorporate value systems and the need for integrating into a larger society. Teachers may also need to be given training on how to handle special needs of ex-child combatants, IDPs, orphans, the disabled, etc.

In order to ensure that the students in the conflict affected areas are given the education that they deserve, the government needs to allocate more funds. Sri Lanka's investment in education is the lowest from the middle income countries.[4] Total spending on education as a percentage of GDP amounts to 1.9 per cent of GDP, whereas in 2005, this figure was 2.6 per cent.[5] Therefore it is evident that the spending on education needs to rise, not only to educate those in the conflict affected areas, but also to improve the quality of education in Sri Lanka as a whole.

## Employment and Skills Development

Decades of war have severely affected employment opportunities in the conflict ravaged areas. According to the Sri Lanka Foundation for

[4] http://www.ft.lk/2011/09/27/invest-in-education/

[5] http://www.sundayobserver.lk/2011/12/25/fin02.asp

Rehabilitation of the Disabled (SLFRD), an estimated 10-15 % of the over 1.1 million population of the Northern Province is estimated to be physically handicapped.[6] It is therefore a challenge to look for employment opportunities for everyone in these areas.

The labour participation rate for the Eastern Province is 41. 5 %. This is lower than that of the rest of the country which stands at 49.5 %. The unemployment rate among women and educated individuals in the Eastern Province is much higher than the rest of the country, suggesting lack of work opportunities in the region. In addressing these issues, policy makers face several challenges.

It is important that investments in education and skills development are geared to generate skills that are in demand in these areas. Such investments must be made equitably and speedily; delays could give rise to new conflicts within these communities. Measures must be taken to re-develop the business environment, in order to create long-term employment opportunities. This involves attracting private sector investments which have, thus far, proved difficult.

In addition to replacing infrastructure, there is a need for investing in new technologies (and training users of the technology to use them) in order to ensure competitiveness in the market place. Furthermore, a process of training and providing employment to those who are disabled and willing to work should be arranged, as they too can contribute towards the economy. A lack of employment and education data makes assessing progress difficult. Thus, there is a significant need for monitoring and evaluation processes in these areas.

## Health

Sri Lanka has been able to maintain overall health indicators at a satisfactory level despite its economic downturns over time. However, there are regional disparities in health indicators and they are compounded in the conflict affected districts.

---

[6] http://www.globalissues.org/news/2011/12/18/12255

Selected health indicators for the North and East have been tabulated below. The disparity between these areas and the country as a whole is evident.

| | Mortality rate 1000 live births in 2000 | Rate per 1000 live births in 2000 | Low birth weight in 2001 | Under-weight in 2002 | Home deliveries in 2001 | Safe sanitation in 2001 |
|---|---|---|---|---|---|---|
| Sri Lanka | 11.2 | 14 | 16.7 | 29.4 | 4 | 72.6 |
| North and East | 14.7 | 81 | 25.7 | 46.2 | 19.4 | 48.2 |
| Ampara | 10.3 | 24 | 22.7 | 44.1 | 19.8 | 52.7 |
| Batticaloa | 15.8 | 117 | 24.3 | 53.2 | 31.4 | 28.4 |
| Trincomalee | 4.6 | 57 | 30.5 | 44.7 | 13.6 | 25.6 |
| Jaffna | 22.3 | 62 | 30.5 | 43.1 | 4.4 | 79 |
| Killinochchi | 27.8 | 158 | NA | NA | NA | NA |
| Mannar | 22.3 | 97 | 12.7 | 38.3 | 39.4 | 70.9 |
| Mulativu | 20.3 | 123 | NA | NA | NA | NA |
| Vavuniya | 8.8 | 76 | 38.8 | 50.6 | 12.3 | 71 |

Source: Department of Census and Statistics.

Significant changes need to be made to the country's health system in order to successfully manage new epidemiological challenges, resulting from the return of IDPs. Therefore, special attention needs to be given to the conflict affected areas.

The government has taken many steps to try to overcome health related issues in the conflict affected areas. The government has also allocated funds under the 'Uthuru Wasanthaya' program, to improve health facilities and has taken steps to develop the main hospital in the Jaffna Peninsula.

However, the government still has major challenges associated with rebuilding hospitals and other health related infrastructure as construction of these buildings often takes a long period of time. The government spending on health has remained static at 1.7 -2 % of GDP. Furthermore, after Sri Lanka's elevation to the status of a middle income country, donor funding has taken a hit, which adversely affects the funds that go into projects that help provide better health care to those in need.

Therefore, there seems to be a need for private sector involvement in health care provisions, but it remains unclear as to how much benefit the poorest people in conflict areas would derive, from private health care.

## Agricultural Development

The three decade long separatist conflict damaged a thriving agricultural sector in the North. The priority given to war led to the neglecting of the agriculture and fishing sectors which were the livelihoods of many people in this province. During the conflict, agricultural goods were also blocked off due to factors such as:

- Government-imposed trade embargoes

- Taxes imposed by the militant groups

- Breakdown of North-South road connectivity and railway

Given the high incidence of poverty among agricultural workers, developments in agriculture are important to the goal of poverty alleviation. It is estimated that over 75 per cent of the rural labour force works in agriculture and that agricultural households represent almost 50 per cent of the poorest households in the country.

With most of the IDPs resettled, the end of the conflict is thus expected to generate increases in demand and supply of agricultural goods in these areas. However, certain challenges lie ahead which need to be addressed.

Coordinated efforts must be made to reduce the agrarian poverty, which stems largely from low resource endowment and skills, poor access to technology and inadequate institutional support. Therefore, there is a need to allocate more finances in order to improve this situation.

Public spending on agricultural research, as a percentage of agricultural GDP, remains low and an increase is needed in order to boost productivity. Public-private partnerships are desirable for this purpose. However, given the difficulties in securing property rights and the public good nature of services, such as surface irrigation, these serve as disincentives to pure private sector investment.

Agricultural land markets are limited in size due to state regulations and ill-defined property rights. This perpetuates the problem of non-viable holdings and short run profitability being prioritised over land sustainability. Thus, the establishment of secure property rights is also an important concern.

Furthermore, inefficiencies in the use of irrigation water need to be addressed. This results from a lack of knowledge of water management strategies and a lack of incentives to save water. A suitable participatory management is required to remedy this.

Productivity in the North and East agricultural sector is low. This is due to capital shortages, credit constraints, lack of access to agricultural inputs and technology and persistently low levels of agricultural research. Therefore, adequate funding and introduction of cutting-edge technology in agriculture is required in order to boost productivity.

Connectivity between the North and East, with the modern dynamic markets is inhibited due to the poor infrastructure and technological advances. The removal of barriers is desirable in order to induce growth in the agricultural sector. Furthermore, the private sector participation could help to develop value chains but government involvement is necessary in order to ensure that the poorest farmers do not find themselves excluded from such processes.

## Infrastructure Development

Infrastructure development in the North and East is crucial to improve livelihood opportunities in the short-term and for economic growth prospects in the medium and long term. The government has taken initiatives to develop the infrastructure in the war ravaged areas through '*Randora*'- which is a national level infrastructure development project and is complemented by projects such as '*Negenahira Navodya*' and '*Uthuru Wasanthaya*'. The primary focus is on developing harbours, roads, and tanks. The government has planned to spend more than US$ 21 billion, over the next 5 years, to improve the infrastructure. This is about 6.5 per cent of the GDP each year.[7]

Foreign assistance is given mostly to develop infrastructure in post-war Sri Lanka. China and Japan have been the main donor countries and have supported the development of infrastructure. Assistance from multilateral sources such as the ADB and the World Bank has also been significant.

Public financing is proving to be challenging as it is putting pressure on the continuously tight fiscal constraints. Private sector participation has been sluggish. Attempts to forge public-private partnerships rely on the implementation of regulatory reforms to protect or develop a regulatory structure that works out a balance between investors' and consumers' interests. However, the challenge is to figure out how the private sector can be encouraged to invest in infrastructure.

## Expansion on Tourism

The end of the separatist war has created a favourable environment for tourism in Sri Lanka. The availability of the North and East, as potential tourist destinations, creates a range of opportunities for expanding the country's tourism sector. 2010 was a significant year for the tourism sector because the number of tourist arrivals exceeded the target for the year, as more than 800,000 tourists visited the island.[8]

It is important that a strategy be implemented in order to improve this promising tourism industry while ensuring a reduction in the negative externalities caused by it. There are a number of challenges that relevant authorities will have to put some thought into, in this regard.

Tourism is highly dependent on infrastructure, particularly in terms of transportation. The poor quality of transport links to the North and East has

---

[7] "Govt plans $ 21 bn public investment through 2015", *Daily Financial Time*, 16 Nov 2011, available online at http://www.ft.lk/2011/11/16/govt-plans-21-b-public-investment-through-2015/

[8] *The Asian Tribune*, 21 December 2011 http://www.asiantribune.com/news/2011/12/20/sri-lanka-welcomes-800000th-tourist-arrived-year-unprecedented-boom-tourist-industry

been a constraint in this respect. Therefore, better access is necessary to promote these areas as tourist destinations.

There is a need for sustainable tourism as tourism products must be carefully designed in order to prevent social and environmental damage at these newly available sites. This could be a good opportunity to boost employment in these areas and also improve the livelihoods of the people living in the areas.

It may be desirable to follow the example of post-war Cambodia and adopt community based tourism. This can promote rural development and facilitate resource conservation in conflict-affected areas.

Focus should also be on attracting high spenders as opposed to only looking at the number of tourist arrivals in the country. Therefore, tourist destinations should also be marketed to such an audience.

## Industrial Development

The growth of the share of industry in Sri Lanka's GDP has been modest over the years. It has increased from 26 per cent in 1990 to 29.7 per cent in 2009. This is partly due to the volatile political and security environment that prevailed during the conflict. These uncertainties acted as a disincentive for private investment, particularly to capital intensive industrial investment.

The post conflict environment has increased opportunities for industrialisation. This was evident when Sri Lanka received its highest ever FDI in 2011, of close to US $1 billion, which is almost double the $516 million received in 2010.

At present, most of the large industrial production facilities are located in the Western Province. However, a number of Export Processing Zones and Industrial Estates have now been established to enable the expansion of industry to other regions as well areas, including the North and East. Achchuveli Industrial Zone in Jaffna is being developed in order to enable small and medium enterprises to better tap the post-war opportunities and is to be opened by mid 2012.[9]

---

[9] *The Daily News*, 9 Nov 2011 http://www.dailynews.lk/2011/09/09/bus04.asp

The current policy framework gives special attention to developing the small and medium enterprise (SME) sector. SMEs will be the key to developing the North and East and can make an important contribution to the domestic economy. However, there are certain challenges that need to be addressed in order to ensure a conducive economic environment for entrepreneurs.

- ▶ Ensuring affordable finance and providing microfinance initiatives, especially in  order to take advantage of untapped capacity in small scale agriculture and fisheries related industries.

- ▶ Providing adequate channels that provide market access would be important to encourage people to start producing goods. Perhaps a dedicated economic centre could be set up in these areas for agro produce, like the one in Dambulla, in order to tap market potential in other regions.

The people in these areas should be made aware of the opportunities on offer and all incentives given so that they can make the most of it.

## Environmental and Natural Resource based Challenges

The conflict has resulted in a depletion of natural resources and has damaged the environment. Failure to address these post conflict issues could impede the achievements of long-term economic goals.

The ill effects on the environment and natural resources have severe repercussions on agriculture, fisheries and tourism, all of which are of potential significance to the North and East. Further, there are landmines and booby traps that still lie around in these areas which are a threat to the lives of those living in these areas. However, the necessary steps seem to have been taken in terms of alerting the public in these areas and continual efforts are taking place in the demining process.[10]

There are some other issues that need to be addressed in order to protect the environment and preserve the natural resources left in the war

---

[10] http://www.onlanka.com/news/land-mine-free-sri-lanka-army-launches-mine-awareness-programme-at-nagarkovil-in-jaffna.html

ravaged areas. Appropriate safeguard measures should be implemented to prevent the over-exploitation of natural resources.

There is a need to reestablish the control of local regulatory bodies and government agencies in order to assess the damage that has been done and to ensure sustainable resource management. These local authorities can also help rehabilitate livelihoods by promoting the sustainable use of environmental resources. The role of the local communities could also be strengthened in environmental resource management.

Resettling original users of resources and reinstating their rights are crucial as to prevent conflict among the people in the area. Therefore, the government can intervene and provide processes that will address the relevant livelihood sustainability issues.

## Concluding Remarks

The multi-dimensional economic challenges in the Northern and Eastern provinces are gradually being addressed. Nearly three years after the war, considerable progress has taken place in the economies of these two provinces. However, there remains a huge unfinished agenda and a number of challenges that need to be addressed by designing sector-specific economic policies and mobilisation of financial resources from donors and the Tamil Diaspora. A political solution (based on the 13th Amendment to the Sri Lankan Constitution) to North and East can assist the economic development programs as it will generate goodwill among the Tamil Community and give a sense of ownership to the ongoing development programs in the conflict-affected areas. Economic policies alone will not be adequate to develop and integrate the conflict-affected areas with the rest of the Sri Lankan economy and this is the political challenge that has to be addressed without further delay.

# Resettlement and Development in Northern Sri Lanka: Conflict to Stabilty

**8**

S B Divaratne

## Introduction

The terrorism that ravaged Sri Lanka for over a quarter of a century devastated the economic network and social fabric of the entire Northern Province. As a result, the Northern Province lost a quarter of a century of development. The development momentum spread over the other parts of the country could not reach the North due to terrorism. Consequently, economic framework of the region was shattered; the agricultural base which is the main source of livelihood for the Northern people was almost ruined. The irrigation sector which provided water for main paddy cultivation through its large network of major, medium and minor tanks was destroyed. All basic infrastructure, which includes road networks including access roads, water supply, irrigation canals etc., had been neglected. Whatever little resources were available were used to strengthen the LTTE warfare and its military installations. The social infrastructure, particularly, schools and hospitals were used to accommodate military cadres of the LTTE. Most of these areas were without power supply and every attempt to provide electricity was thwarted by the LTTE administration. The available infrastructure equipment including telecommunication facilities were used to enhance its capacity at different levels. The Northern Province suffered immensely in terms of economic and social development and it had very little to contribute to national GDP of the country.

Consequent to the victory over terrorism in 2009, the Government of Sri Lanka (GoSL) faced an enormous task of accommodating and caring for nearly 292,000 internally displaced persons (IDPs) and restoring basic infrastructure prior to commencement of the resettlement of IDPs. It had to face twin challenges of de-mining operations and restoration of basic infrastructure in order to ensure safe and sound resettlement program.

This was, by far, the most challenging task ever to have been confronted by any successive government, since Independence. It had to face challenges both internally and externally. The attempts of the Government for rapid resettlement of the IDPs were misinterpreted to discredit the Government. The GoSL knew that a successful program of resettlement is a pre-curser to other important policy initiatives required to resolve the conflict.

**Strategy for Resettlement and Development of the Northern Province**

**Appointment of a *"Presidential Task Force for Resettlement, Development and Security in the Northern Province"* (PTF)**

The strategy of the GoSL stemmed from the policy initiatives introduced by the Government from the very beginning of the resettlement process. Considering the gravity of the situation and the need for a rapid resettlement program and its efficient implementation, the President appointed a Presidential Task Force for Resettlement, Development and Security in the Northern Province (PTF) in May 2009, under the Chairmanship of Basil Rajapaksa, Minister for Economic Development. The mission of the PTF was to formulate a strategic framework for the revitalisation of the Northern Province and to implement a rapid resettlement and recovery program.

The appointment of the TF was a vital policy instrument which set the road map to formulate a strategic framework for a rapid resettlement and recovery program. The initiatives undertaken by the PTF, through its strategic plans, contributed immensely to the success of the resettlement process. The PTF was entrusted with the following tasks:

- To prepare strategic plans, programs and projects to resettle internally displaced persons, rehabilitate and develop economic and social infrastructure of the Northern Province;

- To coordinate activities of the security agencies of the Government in support of resettlement, rehabilitation and development;

- To direct and oversee the implementation of the said plans, programs and projects of the relevant state organisations, including the relevant provincial authorities

- To liaise with all organisations in the public and private sectors and civil society organisations, for the proper implementation of the programs and projects;

- To seek, identify and apply innovative solutions to problems and constraints confronted in the execution of the mandate of the Task Force;

- To regularly review the progress of the implementation of the said programs and projects and to take immediate corrective actions where necessary.

The decision taken by the PTF for rapid resettlement and setting the road map for it through appropriate policy initiatives has been the hallmark of success of the resettlement process. Identifying priorities through well coordinated plans, commissioning of the 180-Day Program, conducting frequent district level meetings to assess and plan out different phases of resettlement, resource mobilisation, etc. were all important initiatives of the PTF to achieve this task.

## Approach

In view of the magnitude of the task, the PTF developed a three-pronged approach for resettlement and development of the 30 year, war-torn Northern Sri Lanka and given the best attention for its implementation using domestic resources as well as external assistance.

## These were:-

i. Providing humanitarian assistance for the resettled people and restoration of basic infrastructure in the cleared area;

ii. Early recovery process to support returnees to recommence their economic activities;

iii. Pursuing the parallel development of much needed major infrastructure and to revive the Northern Region towards sustainability and stability.

The program that envisaged this three-pronged approach was named "*Uthuru Vasanthaya*" (*Vadakkin Vasantham*).

## Humanitarian Assistance

The GoSL decided to accommodate civilian population who were rescued from LTTE in suitable accommodations as a temporary arrangement, as most of the villages were heavily mined. It was also known that most of the LTTE combatants left the LTTE at the last moment and merged with the civilian population to be rescued by the government forces.           Hence, the families were initially accommodated in several Welfare Centres and the majority of them, in the relief villages, set up in Manik farm in Vavuniya District. The facilities at Manik Farm welfare centres took many forms. Every welfare relief village had shelters, referral hospitals, primary health care centres, schools, child care centres, kitchens, tube wells, water tanks, vocational training centres, welfare shops, banks and the post offices.

## Facilities and Maintenance of Welfare Centres

## Accommodation

It was the intention of the Government to provide good accommodation for the IDPs. Initially, semi- permanent shelters were put up by GoSL in Welfare Villages (cemented floors, corrugated and cadjan roofs) to accommodate more than 25,000 people. Several agencies that had received international funding did not respond positively to the call for assistance to build such shelter, claiming that it was expensive. They were also weary that these types of semi-permanent shelters may be used to house IDPs for long period of time. These agencies expressed that they did not wish to assist with what might turn out to be long term housing. UNHCR then took the lead in providing facilities that would last only for three months, with the provision that they would upgrade if these were required for longer periods. With a large influx of IDPs in April and May, tents were made available by UNHCR and other agencies, including in particular, International Organisation for Migration (IOM), catering to a very large influx of IDPs. Each Relief Village was divided into blocks of shelters which had their own kitchens, toilets, water points, tube wells, bathing places and child friendly spaces. These facilities were progressively developed. Special priorities were given for public areas and recreational activities within the centres. Shelters were provided with electricity. Toilets and water points were located within an accessible distance.

## Water

At the beginning, around twenty litres of water per person per day was provided for drinking, cooking and other purpose by bowsers, pumps and tube wells. Identifying the additional need for bathing and washing purposes, water supply was subsequently increased to forty litres / person / day, through pipelines from Malwathu Oya and Kallaru intake. Separate bathing areas for women were specifically constructed. A water treatment plant was built on the banks of Malwathu Oya, to supply drinking water. The absence of water borne and water related epidemics in the Welfare Villages, shows the adequacy of water and sanitation facilities provided. Notwithstanding the overall financial constraints of responding agencies, the water provided, met and exceeded the SPHERE Standard of 7.5-15 litres, adopted by the WHO, as a standard of emergency situations.

## Sanitation

Sri Lankan standards for sanitation were maintained to meet sanitary requirements, with support of the Water and Sanitation cluster, led by UNICEF. Initially, many IDPs were identified with water and sanitation related communicable diseases such as Hepatitis A, Diarrhoea and Typhoid etc. With the improvement of the supply of water and sanitation facilities, all communicable diseases were controlled.

## Food and Nutrition

At the beginning, all the families were fed with cooked meals, as there were no facilities for cooking. But, within a couple of weeks, community kitchens were built in each residential block and community cooking commenced with a generous donation of kitchen utensils by the Government of India. Individual family cooking was introduced as the next step. The World Food Program (WFP) issued IDPs with basic rations and NGOs provided complementary food. In each of the villages, cooperative outlets (Sathosa) were established for the supply of supplementary food items. It must be mentioned that throughout this period, plenty of food, non-food items and other relief materials were brought by people all over the island, for distribution among the IDPs, demonstrating the generosity and magnanimity inherent in Sri Lankan people to support fellow citizens at times of despair and difficulty. Nutritional surveys were carried out and children identified with malnutrition were directed to Nutrition and Rehabilitation Program (NRP) centres for complementary and supplementary feeding and, if needed, therapeutic feeding programs. The high malnutrition rates recorded at the time of rescue were brought down to 13 per cent by December 2009, which is lower than the national average.

## Healthcare

The Ministry of Health developed a master plan and took over the entire mission of providing health services for the IDPs. A Directorate of IDP Health care was established at Manic Farm. In each welfare village, there were Primary Health Care Centres (PHCC) and Referral Hospitals. Each referral hospital was well equipped with: an Emergency Unit, separate male and female wards and an emergency labour room. For the patients to reach the hospital within the Welfare Village, special three wheeler ambulance (Tuk-Tuk Ambulance) services were provided.

All the referral hospitals and PHCC had access to CDMA phone facilities for communication. A pool of ambulances with specially trained Emergency Medical Technicians (EMTs) was on standby at all times to transport patients to secondary and tertiary medical facilities for specialised care. Special mental health clinics were conducted to address mental health issues as well as to support individuals with Post Traumatic Stress Disorder. Artificial limbs for amputees and disabled persons were provided (Prosthetics and Orthotics).

## Psychosocial Work and Recreation

Psychosocial support was made available to all those IDPs who needed such support. The Ministry of Social Services in partnership with Ministry of Health and with the support of UNICEF, conducted a series of psychosocial counselling programs and special programs for elders and persons with special needs. Psychosocial Centres with televisions, computers, books, drawing materials, CD players and musical instruments for children were available. Spaces were made available for extracurricular activities such as Cricket and Volleyball. More than 35,000 individuals were re-united with their families within the welfare villages.

## Education

Schools were established in all the main IDP centres from grade 1 – 11. Special Advanced Level (grade 12 and 13) classes were conducted at the Kadiragamar Village and Advanced Level students from other IDP villages were provided transport to attend these classes. Pre-schools were also established in each of the Relief Villages. There were 49 schools and 100 units for pre-school activity, which is a higher ratio than in the rest of the country. In each welfare village, a Zonal Education Director was appointed to coordinate and facilitate all educational activities. Principals were appointed in each school. The examination department established 10 special examination centres in Vavuniya for 1263 candidates for the Advanced Level Examination held in August 2009. In addition, 166 ex-LTTE child soldiers sat for that examination.

## Vocational Training/ Self Employment

Vocational training centres were established in each of the welfare villages for capacity building and empowerment. Motor mechanical skills, sewing, computing, carpentry lessons etc., were taught at these centres.

**Religious, Spiritual and Cultural Activities:** Places for religious worship were established at all welfare villages. In particular, the Hindu priesthood played a significant role in providing spiritual support for the populace. They were located, as requested, in a separate location and provided with special facilities such as cemented floors. Temples conducted pujas every morning and evening. Special pujas were held for Deepavali and other religious festivals. Masses were conducted on Sundays and on Fridays, there were prayers in the mosque.

**Banking facilities:** The welfare villages were provided with substantial banking facilities for the IDPs, who were able to bring their valuable belongings. They were able to deposit their money, jewellery and gold securely. Both state and private banks were established in the welfare villages, including Bank of Ceylon, People's Bank, National Savings Bank, Seylan Bank, Sampath Bank and Commercial Bank. A mobile banking system was also in operation.

**Registration and providing Identity Cards, Birth and Death Certificates:** An administrative system was put in place, making use of the services of government servants in the centres. Through this system, IDPs were provided with replacements for lost documents such as identity cards, birth and death certificates. Additional support for this was obtained from International Organisation for Migration (IOM). Grama Niladharis within the centres were provided with bicycles to facilitate their work. Communication systems and Post Offices were established in every village, a total of 61 altogether. Publications distributed included newsletters, hand bills, handouts, posters and newspapers. Community Centres with televisions and radios were also established.

**Women and Child Protection:** Care for women and children were given the utmost importance, and in particular, providing protection against gender based violence, domestic violence and child abuse. Services were provided by the Ministry of Child Development and Women's Empowerment and the National Child Protection Authority. The police, the Ministry of Social Services and the Ministry of Health also played a major role. The Ministry of Child Development and Women's Welfare established Units to assist with issues related specifically to women and children. These Units were administered by Tamil speaking female police officers and were designed to provide a facility that provided privacy to the complainant. Complaints with regard to children were addressed to medical personnel who took prompt remedial action. A police post was established in each welfare village with an Inspector and a Sub-Inspector in charge of the Police Post. Complaint books were also made available at each administrative office if the IDPs felt that their rights were violated and complaint boxes were also placed within the welfare villages. Three hundred and sixteen orphaned children aged from one to fourteen were brought under judicial supervision of the Vavuniya Magistrate and were handed into the care of orphanages in Mannar and Vavuniya. A new orphanage was established in Vavuniya. An SOS village was also opened in each welfare village for unaccompanied children. Arrangements were made by Government, with judicial permission, for many of these children to be sent to St. John's College, Jaffna, for education and care.

**Rehabilitation of Ex LTTE Combatants:** A considerable number of the surrendered were active combatants of the LTTE. They were identified through a series of interviews and confessions. Considering the circumstances under which most of them were made combatants and realising the need to reintegrate them with the civilian society, a suitable rehabilitation program was immediately implemented. 11,646 combatants surrendered and opted to go through a rehabilitation program. The rehabilitation program was formulated, taking into consideration, the needs of the surrendered combatants. The rehabilitation focussed on six main areas; namely enhancing the spiritual, cultural and religious practices, providing education for those who were compelled to leave schools, providing basic ICT knowledge, language training, typing and shorthand, vocational training to make them employable, development of skills, need for reintegration with the families and the society and psychosocial and creative therapies. Approximately 9,000 persons, including child combatants have been reintegrated and just over 2,700 remain within the rehabilitation process.

## Formulation of a Master Plan - *"Uthuru Vasanthaya"*

## Launching of a 180-day Accelerated Program

The objectives of the 180-day Program were to identify priorities through well coordinated plans, enlisting support from Line Ministries to undertake activities that were required to create a conducive environment for resettlement and to plan out different phases of resettlement. Each district of the Northern Province had its own program under *Uthuru Vasanthaya,* following guidelines of the PTF, which included priority work to be undertaken during 180-day Programme.

A team of officials was appointed to visit the areas to assess the damage and prepare tentative estimates and to identify fund requirements. Thereafter, priorities were identified for immediate rehabilitation and provision, which include Civil Administration (Kachcheries, Divisional Secretarial offices),

Agriculture infrastructure (Agrarian Service Centres), Education (Schools), Health Services (Hospitals) and Consumer facilities (Co-operatives). Technical capacities of Government Institutions were utilised to complete these renovations within a short space of time. Funds available under on going Projects were utilised to complete this work.

Launching of a 180-day Program brought about total solutions required for rapid resettlement and early recovery process. It includes accelerated de-mining operations, reconstruction of basic infrastructure, provision of humanitarian assistance, water & sanitation and livelihood for early recovery process. All line Ministries were requested to participate in this program and to contribute without any delay, to support the rapid resettlement process. The total solution brought forward through implementation of 180-day Programme included:

- Access to services
- Access to roads, safe drinking water and sanitation, minor irrigation & electricity
- Improvements to basic infrastructure
- Health and education
- Livelihood development

The 180-day program provided the base for identification and planning of resettlement and development programme of the Northern Province. Some of those activities commenced during the 180-day programme.

## Humanitarian Phase of Resettlement

The tasks that were required for creating a conducive environment, to facilitate rapid resettlement, were identified during the formulation of the 180-day Program. The PTF, in association with District Secretaries and the Provincial Authorities, monitored every phase of implementation of activities that were carried out during this phase.

## Twin Challenges

### De-mining

The biggest contribution made by the GoSL in post conflict reconstruction efforts was in the field of de-mining operation. Humanitarian De-mining Unit (HDU) under Sri Lanka Army was set up, with a considerable investment on procurement of de-mining equipment. The Sri Lanka Army contributed greatly in the implementation of a rapid resettlement program, within a short space of time, in addition to the work of several donor-funded, mine action agencies. In order to support the mine action program, the Cabinet officially approved the establishment of a National Mine Action Coordinating Body. Subsequently, the National Mine Action Centre was set up with the assistance of UNDP. The HDU played the lead role and was responsible for nearly 75 per cent of the total cleared area. As on April 2011, 1,170,642,293 sq. metres have been cleared for de-mining operations. This reflects the commitment of the GoSL to free Sri Lanka from the threat of land mines. Considering the need for augmenting the capacity, the GoSL purchased 15 de-mining flail machines, 500 metal detectors and other de-mining equipment, within a short period of time and accelerated the de-mining of identified resettlement areas, access roads, locations of infrastructure and the paddy lands. In addition, in response to a GoSL request, donor agencies procured an additional six flail machines. Manual de-mining capacity of the HDU has been increased up to 1,200, with both Government funds and some assistance from donors and was fully equipped to undertake the humanitarian de-mining operations.

Initially, 5,521,301,137 square metres, in all five districts of the Northern Province, were suspected (unconfirmed) to be contaminated with land mines and unexploded ordnances (UXOs). However, de-mining operations were continued only after the areas were confirmed as hazardous areas after a technical survey. The prioritisation of de-mining operations were as follows:

- Areas required for the resettlement of people;

- Land where people conduct their livelihood activities;

- Land giving access to schools, hospitals, temples/churches;

- Land with essential infrastructure that requires repair, such as existing roads, electricity supply, water supply and irrigation systems;

- Hazardous areas within three kilometres from villages, main roads and access roads;

- Land required for development and construction of new infrastructure;

- Protective minefield around existing military installations;

- Hazardous areas between three and five kilometres from villages, main roads and access roads;

- Hazardous areas within jungles with no direct impact on the daily activities and requirements of the population and authorities;

- Hazardous areas further than five kilometres from villages, main roads and access roads.

### Extent De-mined in Square Metres

| District | Battle Area Clearance (sq metres) | Mine Field Clearance (sq metres) | Non Technical Surveys (sq metres) | Total in (sq metres) |
|---|---|---|---|---|
| Jaffna | 19,635,033 | 4,004,481 | 4,361,600 | 28,001,114 |
| Killinochchi | 20,962,043 | 3,238,420 | 544,585,539 | 568,786,002 |
| Mullathivu | 128,864,253 | 6,937,611 | 0 | 135,801,864 |
| Vavuniya | 68,141,826 | 3,955,356 | 95,829,986 | 167,927,168 |
| Mannar | 174,669,335 | 12,581,339 | 82,875,471 | 270,126,145 |
| Total | 412,272,490 | 30,717,207 | 727,652,596 | 1,170,642,293 |

Source: Ministry of Planning

The Sri Lanka Army (SLA) played a major role in this endeavour. The HDU of SLA cleared a considerable extent of land during the period. Around 545 square kilometres of Battle Area Clearance out of 760 square kilometres is by HDU of SLA. About 727 square kilometres were cleared through Non Technical Surveys (NTS). The major performers in NTS are Danish De-mining Group (DDG), HDU of SLA and Sarvatra. The NGOs who participated in de-mining activities were Halo Trust, DDG, Mines Adversary Group (MAG), Swiss Foundation of Mine Action (FSD), Horizon, Sarvatra and Milinda Moragoda Institute for People's Empowerment.

## Restoration of Basic Infrastructure

Prior to commencement of the resettlement, the GoSL spearheaded the rapid rehabilitation of infrastructure through its 180-day Program. Initially, priority was given to essential infrastructure (i.e. access roads, minor tanks, public buildings to facilitate delivery mechanism, hospitals, schools, Agrarian Services Centres, Divisional Secretary Offices etc.) and the full responsibility for restoration and reconstruction was undertaken by the Government agencies (i.e. Central Engineering Consultancy Bureau (CECB), State Development and Construction Corporation (SD&CC) and State Engineering Corporation (SEC). The GoSL invested approximately Rs. 6.6. billion (US$ 59.44 million) to procure earth moving and construction machinery and equipment required for reconstruction and development of infrastructure. The Ministry of Nation Building and Estate Infrastructure Development (presently the Ministry of Economic Development) spent nearly Rs. 4.4 billion (US$ 39.63 million) for rehabilitation of infrastructure identified as priorities under the 180-day Program. Furthermore, through the "*Gama Neguma*" (Village Development) program of the Ministry of Economic Development, considerable investment has been made since 2006, for improvement of several sectors under infrastructure and for social development.

## Status of Resettlement

Except for 2,268 families, all others who were accommodated in the welfare centres have now been resettled in their places of origin. These families are unable to return to their villages as they were heavily mined.

### Status of Resettlement as on July 2011

| District | Resettled Families | Resettled Persons |
|---|---|---|
| Mannar | 22,191 | 86,220 |
| Mullaitivu | 23,740 | 71,176 |
| Jaffna | 35,178 | 107,836 |
| Vavuniya | 10,416 | 36,037 |
| Kilinochchi | 37,671 | 120,943 |
| **Total** | 129,196 | 422,212 |

Source: Ministry of Planning

## Every resettled family was provided with the following assistance:

- Provision of dry rations ;

- Initial grant of Rs. 5,000 as part of a total Shelter Grant of Rs.25, 000 ;

- Land preparation cost of Rs. 4000 per acre ;

- Non Food Relief Items (NFRI); mosquito nets, Jerrycans, kitchen sets, towels, plastic mats, bedsheets, plastic basins, GI buckets ;

- Additional NFRI on need basis; clothing, coconut scrapers, slippers, food containers, tarpaulin kits; plastic sheets (4 x 5 m), nylon ropes ;

- Hygiene packs as per UNICEF standards;

- Return tool kits; crow bar, axe, rake, heavy carpenter hammer, shovel, mammoty, hurricane lamp, jungle knife ;

- Provision of paddy seed (2 bushels per acre per family for two acres) ;

- Roofing sheets (12 nos. per family);

- Cement bags (8 nos. per family).

## Shelter

The first priority in resettlement process was to provide shelter. A survey carried out by the district staff and the security personnel observed that housing had been a critical issue even when this area was under the LTTE control. Major cause for the damage was removal of roofs, doors and windows as the LTTE instructed people to remove whatever possible and retreat with the LTTE so that the people can construct new houses at new locations.

The rest had been living in temporary houses made out of perishable materials and hence were totally destroyed, by the time resettlement commenced. During the period 2005 – 2008, North East Housing Reconstruction Program (NEHRP) constructed new houses in Killinochchi and Mullathivu districts. However, due to restrictions imposed by the unsecured situation, the total number of houses constructed by NEHRP in Killinochchi and Mullathivu were 611 and 613 respectively.

Action was taken to provide cash grants and shelter materials as an immediate solution for the people, either to repair a part of the damaged houses or to construct temporary types of shelters. On the request of GoSL, a cash grant of Rs. 25,000 was funded by the UNHCR. An advance of Rs. 5,000 was given through the Divisional Secretary and the balance of Rs. 20, 000 through the Bank of Ceylon. In addition, NFRI were distributed, which included two tarpaulin sheets and nylon ropes as tent material. The GoSL provided 12 roofing sheets and eight cement bags with the assistance of the Government of India to make the temporary shelter weatherproof. With this assistance, all the returnee families, as soon as they are resettled, were able to have roofs above their heads.

Simultaneously, a program was launched to upgrade the housing stock to semi-permanent houses, which would last for two to three years or more until permanent houses were provided. These houses were called transitional shelters and the number constructed by now is around 23,000. The model for semi-permanent houses was first introduced by International Organisation of Migration (IOM) through consultation with the PTF. Subsequently, all INGO/ NGOs were directed to put up that model of houses instead of assistance to put up tents.

**Number of Transitional Shelters Constructed**

| District | No. of Transitional (semi-permanent) shelters constructed |
|---|---|
| Jaffna | 5,562 |
| Killinochchi | 5,809 |
| Mullathivu | 4,579 |
| Vavuniya | 1,210 |
| Mannar | 5,716 |
| **Total** | 22,876 |

Source: Ministry of Finance and Planning

## Domestic Water Supply

Most of the wells in the resettled areas were contaminated and damaged when the resettlement commenced and required renovation. Renovation of wells was considered a top priority during the humanitarian phase of resettlement. National Water Supply and Drainage Board (NWS&DB) was entrusted to take lead in this exercise with support from UNICEF. Besides, NGO partners also played a major role in cleaning and reconstruction of dug wells. Nearly 8,421 wells have been cleaned / rehabilitated during this period by the NWS&DB and Water Resources Board (WRB). Further, 9,000 wells have been cleaned with assistance by INGOs. In addition, 92 tube wells have been repaired and 27 have been constructed by the NWS&DB.

The next priority was given to domestic water supply. A policy was adopted to provide at least one well for every five families. Large number of wells were cleaned or renovated during this period. The NWS&DB and the WRB played the main role, financially supported by the UNICEF. The NGOs too undertook renovation and repairs of a large number of dug wells and tube wells. Some wells were cleaned by the people with water pumps supplied for the purpose.

In order to develop water supply schemes, several projects have been undertaken by the GoSL, with its own funds and resources received from ADB and JAICA. The details of which are as follows:

**Water Supply Schemes**

| Project | Funding Agency | Location | Cost (Rs. Mn) |
|---|---|---|---|
| Water Supply Scheme (WSS) | ENReP (GoSL) | Mannar, Vavuniya, Mullaitivu, Jaffna | 1,602.3 |
| | UNICEF | Jaffna, Vavuniya, Mannar, Mullaitivu | 70.88 |
| | ADB | Mannar, Vavuniya, Jaffna, Kilinochchi | 5,700.0 |
| | ADB/IFRC | Jaffna | 600.0 |
| | JICA | Kilinochchi | 772.2 |
| | JICA (2KR) | Northern Province | 260.0 |
| | NWS&DB | Jaffna, Vavuniya | 8.0 |
| Total | | | 9,013.38 |

Source: Ministry of Finance and Planning

## Access and Internal Roads

The major issue pertaining to access and internal roads was contamination with land mines. The HDU of the SLA took the initial step to clear the roads of land mines as a priority. By the time people were brought in, all the roads were passable and free of land mines. Programs were organised to renovate the roads, especially the structures with the support of funds released from on going projects.

## Education

Majority of the schools were damaged in the conflict. Immediately after liberation, a team of technical officers was appointed to visit each and every village and assess the damages to public buildings. Priority was given to school buildings as students had to commence schooling immediately. Where the damages were beyond immediate repairs, temporary school buildings with necessary facilities were put up. Schools were furnished and equipped to commence education. Special efforts were made to provide teachers' / students' furniture by the Provincial Administration. Commendable assistances were provided by INGOs / NGOs to provide furniture for schools. Due to lack of transport facilities for students, arrangements were made by NGOs to supply bicycles.

## Health

The objective of the GoSL was to ensure sustained access to and use of comprehensive health and nutritional services by the population in the areas of return. This included preventive, curative and rehabilitative services. During the period of conflict, the health infrastructure suffered significant damages across the Northern Province. Some of the health institutions had been used as LTTE camps. Concurrently, with the resettlement, action was taken to repair, equip and open several hospitals, clinics and peripheral units, to provide the services to returnees. Ministry of Health, with the support of many NGO partners, implemented programs to improve preventive and curative services, including disease surveillance system and outbreak response, control of vector-borne, food-borne and water-borne diseases; reproductive health, mental and psychosocial services as well as support and care to people with disabilities. A special emphasis was laid, on children's nutrition program and to maintaining the improved nutritional status of the children at the welfare centres.

When the hospitals, clinics and peripheral units were renovated, several donor agencies supported them with medical and other equipment and supplies to strengthen the services at all levels. Transport facilities for patients, including referral to secondary and tertiary facilities and mobility of health workers were enhanced through provision of vehicles, distribution of motorbikes and bicycles for field health workers.

## Early Recovery

The second phase of the humanitarian assistance was directed towards early recovery activities since it became necessary to provide assistance for the returnees to commence their economic operations. They required more attention on activities that would support them to recommence their economic operations. In order to cater to these requirements, the GoSL stepped up interventions and further promoted early recovery initiatives as a further step to revitalise the livelihoods of the resettled families. These included the creation of a supportive environment for the 2010 / 11 agricultural Maha season through the provision of inputs and services to enhance the opportunities for agricultural activities. The GoSL welcomed INGOs / NGOs involvement in effectively building up livelihood of the resettled families. In order to avoid duplication and to ensure optimum use of funding by INGOs / NGOs, PTF issued guidelines & directions and prioritised livelihood activities while continuing attention to shelter requirements, in partnership with donors and other Government entities.

Immediately after the 180-day program, data was collected from Grama Sevaka Divisions to identify immediate needs of the returnees. The data was compiled into an *"Action Plan"* which identified the priority activities to be completed in 2010 and the balance to be completed thereafter. All the implementing agencies including government, UN agencies and NGOs were instructed to identify activities from the action plan. While the humanitarian requirement was looked into, the major focus in 2010 was for early recovery of livelihood development and income generating activities.

Sustainability and durability of the resettlement program was based on re-establishment of livelihood activities. Around 70-80 % of the people in the Northern Province were farmers and 20- 30 % were from the fishing community. A miniscule percentage was engaged in animal husbandry and self employment activities.

Most of INGO / NGOs and some of the UN agencies played an active role in supporting livelihood activities. 39 INGOs were involved in supporting livelihood development activities among the resettled families in all the districts. The principle adopted was to provide grants in cash or kind for resettled families to re-engage in the economic activity that they were involved in, prior to displacement. As a policy, each selected family was provided a package of assistance valued at least Rs. 35,000, so that it will be adequate to meet the initial requirement of any livelihood. The package or combination of more than one package was decided in consultation with each family and identifying their specific skills and needs.

## Paddy Cultivation

The largest economic activity in the Northern Province is paddy farming and the total extent of Paddy lands is recorded as 247,000 acres. The largest extent of paddy cultivation is under major, medium and minor irrigation. Some lands are cultivated in the Maha season under rain fed conditions.

The Agriculture department, in collaboration with the FAO provided seed paddy at the rate of three bushels per acre for all the paddy farmers. The Provincial Department of Agriculture, under the guidance of central and provincial Ministries, implemented the program. In 2010 / 11 Maha, farmers were able to cultivate 210,000 acres of paddy land.

The resettled farmer families faced a serious impediment as there were no tractors or any other farm power to plough and prepare the lands. GoSL negotiated with the Government of India and obtained 500 four wheel tractors to be given to Agrarian Services centres in the North. The GoSL also released funds received from the US Department of Agriculture to procure additional four wheel tractors. NGOs followed the lead given by the donors and provided many two wheel tractors. In fact, today the availability of tractors with the Agrarian Services Centres in the North exceeds the actual need.

It was realised that farmers do not have cash to pay for the operation cost of the tractors at the initial stage. Therefore, arrangements were made to provide cash grants of Rs. 4,000 per acre for the lands cultivated in the first two seasons. Funds were channelled through the Agrarian Services Centres, who had the enhanced capacity to undertake a large extent of land preparation.

There were stray cattle at the beginning of the season and rounding up of cattle was launched with support of the security forces. Considering the need to protect the paddy crop, farmer organisations were supplied with barbed wire for perimeter fencing.

There was a large extent of paddy land abandoned for a period of over 20 years. By 2009, most of them were covered with shrub jungles. Sri Lanka Army with financial assistance provided by the Emergency Northern Recovery Project (ENReP), implemented by the GoSL, undertook the clearing of abandoned paddy lands.

## Highland Cultivation of Other Food Crops

Subsidiary food crops such as Black gram, Green gram, Maize and Ginger are produced in the Northern Province under rain fed conditions. The FAO provided seed materials for farmers to commence rain fed subsidiary food crops cultivation. The Government of India also made arrangements to supply seed materials, mainly groundnuts as well as agricultural implements.

## Cultivation of High Valued Crops with Lift Irrigation

The Northern farmers, especially the farmers in Jaffna peninsula, grow high value crops utilising lift irrigated water. Traditional method used in the past had been replaced with kerosene water pumps. In the mainland where water is available in the streams and food production wells, farmers were practicing lift irrigated cultivation. The crops were mainly chillies, red onion and vegetables. As there was a good market for these crops in adjoining townships as well as in the South, farmers were heavily benefited with high value crop cultivation.

During the period of conflict, the farmers had lost nearly 10,000 water pumps. A special program was launched to supply water pumps to the farmers who had reliable water sources for pumping water. Around 7,500 water pumps were distributed both by NGOs and the Provincial Council.

## Home Gardening

Being a rural region, most of the homesteads in the North are more than half an acre in extent. A program was arranged to develop home gardens with fruit trees, including mangoes and jack, plantation crops such as coconut and Palmyra, timber species and vegetables. The concept embodied in the "*Divi Neguma*" program was adopted in home garden development integrating agriculture with animal husbandry and cottage industries.

## Fisheries

The Northern Province is endowed with large internal water bodies and the coastal belt all around the province. Shallow sea on the West and the lagoons all around Jaffna peninsula made a large percentage of the people, fishermen. The fishing includes inland fisheries, lagoon fishing and deep sea fishing. A special program was launched to assist fishermen to commence fishing activities in all the three sectors.

## Inland Fisheries

There was a project under the Ministry of Fisheries to assist inland fishermen by providing canoes, fishing gear and bicycles with fish boxes. The project was supplemented by the NGOs to ensure adequate number of equipment for inland fisheries.

## Deep Sea and Lagoon Fishing

Similar assistance was extended to lagoon and deep sea fishing through supply of boats, engines, fishing gear and required infrastructure facilities including fisheries cooperative buildings.

Sri Lanka Army (SLA) had collected a considerable number of fishing boats in the Eastern coastal belt. They were heavily damaged during the course of the conflict and abandoned by the fleeing IDPs. The SLA took a special interest and repaired around 65 fishing boats with engines and distributed them among the returning fishermen families.

## Dairy Cattle

In view of the cultural and religious practices of the people of North, no attempt was made to encourage beef cattle. Instead the major thrust was on rearing dairy cattle. Farmers were provided with a cow and a calf and materials for a shed. Milk collecting centres, connected with the main powder milk producers, received a focus under NGO programs. The rounding up of cattle by the SLA increased milk production of the region. The plan of the PTF is to involve around 10 per cent of the families in dairy farming so that family economy will be developed and intake of milk will also be increased to raise the nutritional level.

## Goat Rearing

It was observed that the local population is used to goat farming. With the help of NGOs, a scheme was operated to provide around four female goats to a family. Where animals are available, each family was provided with a male goat as well. There was a shortage of high quality male goats; hence arrangements were made to provide one male animal to five families. The target is to supply goats to 30 per cent of the families as a source of supplementary income.

## Backyard Poultry

A larger percentage of families preferred to have backyard poultry to supplement family income. The PTF took special interest to promote this activity. A considerable number of female headed families are engaged in the backyard poultry program. It is anticipated that around 50 per cent of the families will engage in backyard poultry. The selected families were provided with 15 to 20, one month old chicks and materials for cages with assistance of the GoSL and NGOs.

## Self Employment

A significant number of families are headed by persons employed in small enterprises. Therefore, village level blacksmiths, bicycle repair shops, tailors, and retail shopkeepers, masons and carpenters were also targeted under livelihood development programs.

## Cash for Work

Targeting the poorest of poor, a program was launched for cash for work to rehabilitate rural infrastructure facilities while generating employment for the poor.

## Special Events

### *Joint Plan for Assistance - Northern Province* (JPA) - 2011

A Joint Plan for assistance for the Northern Province in 2010 was prepared through a consultative process led by the GoSL through the Presidential Task Force, for assistance needed during 2011. This process was undertaken jointly with the United Nations and its Agencies and National and International Non-Governmental Organisations (NGOs / INGOs), subsequent to an evaluation of work carried out during 2010 under several sectors. The objective of the JPA was to identify the balance priority activities that must be undertaken during 2011; and it is to facilitate international assistance in order that the people of Northern Province can recover, rebuild and return to a normal life. The ultimate aim of such work is to ensure the long term sustainable development of the Northern Province within the shortest time frame possible.

## Family Profile

The PTF directed all Divisional Secretaries to prepare a family profile of all those families who were resettled, for the purpose of future planning, for development of the resettled families. Guidelines were issued to the Divisional Secretaries with regard to the preparation of the family profile. The collection of data and maintaining of records at the Divisional Secretariat with regard to all resettled families was considered an important exercise to address the needs of resettled families. A complete family profile is now available with the Divisional Secretariat for future planning.

## Restoration of Social and Economic Infrastructure

## Improving Quality of Life

Economic and social infrastructure development is the third phase of the Strategy for reconstruction of the Northern Province. This is an ongoing process which will entail the entire development spectrum of the Northern Province. A massive investment has been set apart for reconstruction of highways, railways, irrigation network, power supply, water supply etc. The investment includes domestic as well as external assistance. The line Ministries have taken over the responsibility of implementing the tasks with special emphasis, in order to complete the work during the scheduled timeframe. It is the belief of the Government that the private sector involvement would be encouraged, based on the development of the infrastructure which would eventually create the necessary environment to encourage private sector involvement in the development phase. It must be noted that the Government has taken upon itself, the responsibility to create the enabling environment for the smooth functioning of the Government machinery and the delivery systems, the private sector participation and also to attract external assistance to reconstruct the Northern Province.

By doing this, the Government has unequivocally demonstrated its sincere commitments to rebuild the Northern Province. The following is a brief description of development activities that have taken place during the past one and half years as a part of the ongoing process towards sustainability and stability.

## Permanent Housing Construction Programme

The majority of houses were partially or totally destroyed during the conflict. In fact, nearly 34,000 families were without proper shelter even when the areas were under de facto LTTE control. To provide shelter to the resettled families has been a tremendous task though the Government cannot take the responsibility to provide shelter to all the resettled families. However, the Government, through its projects with the support from the UN agencies / INGOs, has completed 18,534 permanent houses and 22,876 semi-permanent houses during 2009 / 2010 and till date. Having realised the magnitude of the housing issue, the Government has requested donor support for housing construction.

Consequent to the visit by His Excellency, the President of Democratic Socialist Republic of Sri Lanka, Mahinda Rajapaksa to India, the Government of India (GoI) has pledged its assistance, which is a grant to construct nearly 50,000 housings for North and the East and also estate sector in Sri Lanka. Of this, 38,000 houses have been reserved for the Northern Province, of which, construction of 1,000 houses for landless vulnerable families have already been commenced. In addition, the GoI has undertaken to repair nearly 4,000 houses in the Northern Province.

The total commitment for construction of permanent houses in the Northern Province is as follows:

| Name of the Agency | No. of Housing Units (Committed) | No. of Housing Units (Completed) |
|---|---|---|
| Implemented by NEHRP (GoSL) | 27,392 | 14,292 |
| Under Assistance from the Government of India | 38,000 | (Construction of 1,000 houses already commenced) |
| UNHABITAT | 8,000 | 3,232 |
| European Union | 3,232 | 518 |
| Sri Lanka Red Cross | 2,520 | 492 |
| Total | 79,144 | 18,534 |

Source: Ministry of Finance and Planning

The European Union provided funds to the INGOs, to construct 3,232 permanent houses in Vavuniya District. At the first stage, EU project had completed 518 housing units. The balance will be completed in two years time frame.

GoSL took the leadership by allocating more funds for housing construction under the already on-going North East Housing Reconstruction Project (NEHRP). NEHRP has already completed 14,292 houses in all five districts. Total number of houses to be constructed in 2011 under NEHRP is 13,100, of which a fair number of houses are nearing completion and the balance is in progress. UN Habitat followed the GoSL and agreed to construct 7,900 houses with Australian and EU assistance. Around 3,785 are completed. Many NGOs have expressed their interest to assist returnees in housing. The Sri Lanka Red Cross has taken the lead to construct 2,520 houses in Killinochchi and Mullathivu districts. Around 492 are already completed. Many other NGOs have undertaken small numbers of permanent houses for construction or repairs.

## Restoration of Health and Nutrition

A substantial investment has been made by the GoSL for upgrading of health services which was almost paralysed in the resettled areas. High priority was accorded to renovate primary health care institutions during the 180-Day Program and to improve medical care for the resettled families and to the IDPs in welfare centres. In addition, an extensive work, by engaging in recovery and construction of hospitals, provision of equipment and furniture and functions, deployment of staff, strengthening of surveillance and healthcare delivery services were carried out.

The GoSL carried out the construction of a three-storey surgical operation threatre complex at the General Hospital Mannar; renovated two District General hospitals in Kilinochchi and Mullaitivu districts, two Base hospitals, nine Divisional hospitals, five Primary medical Care Units, four MoH Offices and 20 Gramodaya health Centres (GMC) enabling treatment of over 23,000 patients since November 2009. Structural development of hospital units have also been carried out (i.e. Base Hospitals at Chavakachcheri – Administration Block with OPD and Drugstores, Construction of two MOH Offices in Kayts and Uduvil, Establishment of CSSD and General Hospital Vavunia, Surgical Threatre Complex, District General Hospital Mannar, Construction of PMCU and Thiruketheeswaram, Construction of Blood Bank, DGH Mannar) together with the improvement of accommodation facilities for doctors and health staff (two-storey consultation quarters at Base Hospital Point Pedro, 30 room quarters at DGH Mannar, six unit quarters Vavuniya), eight maternity wards, two Biomedical engineering (M+BME) and Pathology Units.

| Facility | Numbers |
|---|---|
| Preventive Care Institutions | 161 |
| Curative Care Institutions | 91 |
| Chest Clinics | 5 |
| Leprosy Units | 1 |
| STD Clinics | 4 |
| Ayurvedic Medical Institutions | 83 |

Source: Ministry of Health

The GoSL provided medical equipment, hospital furniture, pharmaceuticals and five large generators to the Ministry of Health (MoH) of the Northern Province, supplied 10 large generators to clinics and hospitals, facilitating primary health care activities in Manic Farm. Anti-Malaria Campaign worth Rs. 26 million ($234 million) in 2010, were carried out in all five districts to combat malaria. MoH provided curative health care services to welfare centres to improve the health and nutritional status of the IDPs, which resulted in improvement of maternity care and nutrition and reduction in child morbidity and mortality and maintained a 99 percent coverage for immunisation for infants and pre-school children under National Immunisation Programme.

**Total expenditure by the GoSL**

Rs. Mn.

| District | 2009 | 2010 | 2011 | Total |
|---|---|---|---|---|
| Jaffna | 316.695 | 377.245 | 27.420 | 721.360 |
| Vavuniya | 399.032 | 315.904 | 2.915 | 717.851 |
| Mannar | 250.701 | 251.642 | 11.119 | 513.462 |
| Kilinochchi | 72.948 | 256.059 | 13.812 | 342.819 |
| Mullaitivu | 40.824 | 249.789 | 0.765 | 291.378 |
| PDHS Office | - | 26.173 | - | 26.173 |
| Selected areas in NP | - | - | - | - |
| **Total** | 1,080.20 | 1,476.812 | 56.031 | 2,613.043 |

Source: Ministry of Health

A special project was launched to develop a teaching hospital in Jaffna covering medical, surgical, paediatric, gynaecological and obstetrics needs. The cost of the special project which is already underway amounts to Rs. 3,883.3 million.

**Major Developments - Teaching Hospital, Jaffna**

| Facility | Amount Rs.Mn |
|---|---|
| a. From JICA funds (operation theatre, ICU, Central Laboratory, Central Sterilisation Unit and Supply of Medical equipment)-Improvement of central functions of teaching Hospital Jaffna | 1,877 |
| b. Chinese Government-Emergency Treatment Unit Project (Yet to be implemented | 750 |
| c. Medical Ward Complex | 150 |
| Blood Bank Complex | 25 |
| Kitchen Complex | 20 |
| Lifts, Transformers and other renovations | 61.3 |
| Total | 3,883.3 |

Source: Ministry of Health

## Revival of Education System

Altogether, there are 1,020 schools in the 12 educational zones in the Northern Province. By May 2009, most of the schools except in locations like Jaffna, Mannar and Vavuniya Town were damaged. Many of the school buildings were without roofs. There was no furniture in many of the schools. They were either damaged or removed. During the 180-Day program, major attention was given to repair damaged school buildings and to repair and furnish damaged school buildings. Since 2009, 1,630 school buildings have been repaired at a total cost of Rs. 1,341 million and the entire investment was borne by the GoSL. By now, 1,020 schools are fully functioning in the Northern Province, with a total student population of 260,582 and having the services of 13,967 teachers.

As a part of its development partnership with Sri Lanka and in response to requirements projected by the GoSL, the Government of India has undertaken to repair 79 schools in the Northern Province (Kilinochchi, Mullaitivu and Vavuniya Districts) with the total outlay of SLRS 187 million.

The High Commission of India has awarded the contract to a Sri Lankan construction company and signing of the Contract Agreement has already been accomplished.

### School repair work carried out during the period 2009-2011

| Zone | No. of Schools in each Zone | No of Schools closed in each Zone | No. of Items done | | | |
|---|---|---|---|---|---|---|
| | | | 2009 | 2010 | 2011 | Total |
| Jaffna | 116 | 13 | 39 | 69 | 68 | 176 |
| Vadamarachchi | 82 | 20 | 41 | 46 | 78 | 165 |
| Valikamam | 152 | 07 | 49 | 66 | 52 | 167 |
| Thenmaradchi | 66 | 09 | 21 | 40 | 32 | 93 |
| Islands | 76 | 22 | 27 | 35 | 36 | 98 |
| Kilinochchi | 103 | 13 | 12 | 80 | 92 | 184 |
| Mullaitivu | 55 | 27 | Ñ | 23 | 26 | 49 |
| Thunnukkai | 56 | 01 | 21 | 49 | 68 | 138 |
| Mannar | 78 | 02 | 55 | 44 | 79 | 178 |
| Madhu | 42 | 03 | 14 | 22 | 41 | 77 |
| V/North | 90 | 11 | 14 | 49 | 34 | 97 |
| V/South | 104 | Ñ | 96 | 40 | 72 | 208 |
| **Total** | 1,020 | 128 | 389 | 563 | 678 | 1,630 |

Source: Ministry of Education

## Restoration of Water and Sanitation

People of Northern Province, mostly living in rural areas were dependent on shallow dug wells for their domestic water. The major town centres such as Jaffna, Vavuniya, Kilinochchi and Mannar were provided with water supply schemes, managed by the National Water Supply and Drainage Board (NWS&DB).

These water supply schemes were all renovated by the NWS&DB. Large volumes of work of cleaning of dug wells were completed during the 180-Day program. The water supply in Kilinochchi and Adampan were destroyed by the LTTE. In terms of development priorities, restoration of water supply has been considered another priority area in the development agenda of the Northern Province. The NWS&DB has taken positive steps in this direction and the following work has already been undertaken with a massive investment through loans from donors.

**On-going Projects (Water Supply Scheme)**

| Project | Funding Agency | Location | Cost ( Rs. Mn) |
|---|---|---|---|
| Water Supply Scheme (WSS) | ENReP (GoSL) | Mannar, Vavuniya, Mullaitivu, Jaffna | 1,602.3 |
| | UNICEF | Jaffna, Vavuniya, Mannar, Mullaitivu | 70.88 |
| | ADB | Mannar, Vavuniya | 5,700.0 |
| | | Jaffna, Kilinochchi | 20,000.0 |
| | ADB/IFRC | Jaffna | 600.0 |
| | JICA | Kilinochchi | 772.2 |
| | JICA (2KR) | Northern Province | 260.0 |
| | NWS&DB | Jaffna, Vavuniya | 8.0 |
| **Total** | | | 29,013.38 |

Source: Ministry of Finance and Planning

## Restoration of Electricity

Consequent to the liberation of the Vanni District, restoration of electricity facilities and electrification was considered a top priority to facilitate resettlement and commercial activities. Due to destruction caused to main power transmission line between Vavuniya and Chunnakan, the power supply to Jaffna was provided through a network of Ceylon Electricity Board (CEB) and the private suppliers. However, most of the areas of the Northern Province were without electricity supply for many years. The policy of the Government under Uthuru Vasanthaya is to provide 100 per cent coverage of electricity to the Northern Province. During 2009 and 2010, Ministry of Power and Energy completed 2,033 tasks at a cost of Rs 1,497 million. A major achievement in electricity was supply of power to Kilinochchi and Mullaitivu. Another important achievement was supply of power to the Kokkavil radio transmission tower.

**Comparison of Electrification Level**

| District | June-2009 (Before commencing the project) | Today |
|----------|-------------------------------------------|-------|
| Vavuniya | 62% | 75% |
| Mannar | 37% | 60% |
| Kilinochchi | 0% | 27% |
| Mullaithivu | 0% | 23% |
| Jaffna | 60% | 79% |

Source: Ministry of Finance and Planning

**On-going Projects**

| Description | Project Cost Rs. Mn |
|---|---|
| Vavuniya - Kilinochchi transmission line to provide electricity to Vavuniya, Kilinochchi and Mullaithivu Districts funded by JICA | 3747.0 |
| Kilinochchi -Chunnakam transmission line to provide power to Jaffna and Kilinochchi Districts funded by ADB | 3122.4 |
| Augmentation of Vavuniya Grid Station, funded by the CEB (ESCROW) | 265.0 |
| Uthuru Wasanthaya 100% electrification of Northern Province Project Allocation for short term measures funded by the GoSL & CAARP/ADB | 1200.0 |
| Allocation for medium term measures funded by the ESCROW A/C | 5297.0 |

Source: Ministry of Finance and Planning

## Path to Spiritual Development

Concerted effort was made to renovate religious places, mainly Hindu temples, Catholic churches and mosques with investment by the Government, through the Department of Hindu Religious and Cultural Affairs.

### The following Hindu Temples were renovated:

### Thiruketheesvaram Temple

This Temple is a pre-historic sacred kovil in Manthoddam, in the Mannar District. The area became inaccessible to the pilgrims due to LTTE terrorism and was also abandoned. After the liberation, action was initiated by GoSL with the assistance of the GoI, for restoration of this temple. The GoSL spent approximately Rs.75 million for development of access roads and internal road systems. The Restoration Society of the Kovil with the assistance of GoI is making arrangements to restore the granite pillars at a cost of Rs.200 million.

The following temples were renovated through special financial assistance, granted by the Department of Hindu Religious and Cultural Affairs:

- Thirumurukandi Kovil in Mullaitivu District

- Naguleshwaram Kovil in Jaffna

- Vallipuram Alwa Kovil in Point Pedro, Jaffna

- Nagapooshari Amman Kovil Nainativu

- Maviddapuram Kandswamy Temple in Jaffna

- Vattapalai Amman Temple in Mullaitivu District

- Silva Sannidhi Murugan Temple in Wadamarachchi, Jaffna

- Kanthaswamy Temple in Kilinochchi

- Thanthonries Warar Temple in Oddusudanm Mullaitivu District

## Renovation of Shrine of Our Lady of Madhu

The shrine of Our Lady of Madhu is the main Catholic Marian Shrine in Mannar which has a history of over 400 years. It is the centre for pilgrimage and worship for Sri Lankan Catholics. The LTTE cadres occupied the church premises and had weapons placed in the area, set up road blocks and prevented pilgrims entering the area. The renovation of the church was fully carried out by the Sri Lanka Army in 2009 and the GoSL spent Rs.447.3 million for improvement of the church.

## Muslim Religious Places

The following religious places were renovated by the Government Muslim Religious Cultural Affairs: Jumma Mosque in Mannar, Jumma Mosque in Nanaddan, 5 Jumma Mosques in Manthai West, 17 Jumma Mosques in Cheddikulam, Vavuniya

## Restoration of Administration

The administration in Kilinochchi and Mullaitivu districts was completely paralysed during the latter stages of the conflict. The Government was able to maintain civil administration, despite the fact that both districts were under de-facto control of the LTTE for several years. The public service was maintained and paid for by the Government. It had to work under duress since they were forced to carry out the LTTE Agenda. Even during later stages of the war, skeleton staff of the public service was in service to distribute the food among the civilians held hostage by the LTTE and maintain health services. Establishment of administration prior to the resettlement was considered the most important priority since the delivery of services to the resettled families had to be channelled through the public service. Restoration of administration by reconstruction of the District Secretariats, Divisional Secretariat Office and other institutions such as Agrarian Services Centres, cooperatives, hospitals and schools were given priority in the 180-Day accelerated program. By the time the resettlement took place, the Government was able to have the most important public offices rehabilitated and opened to facilitate the delivery system.

## Growth Initiatives

## Revival of Agriculture

Agriculture is the most vital economic sector and a source of livelihood for 80 per cent of the population in the Northern Province that provided basic food security in the Province. The revival of agriculture commenced with restoration of the entire irrigation system, cleaning of abandoned paddy lands, supply of inputs and agriculture machinery that were required for immediate revival of the agriculture. The GoSL made considerable investment on revival of agriculture sector. Concerted efforts were made to bring back abandoned paddy lands under cultivation. These lands, having been neglected for many years, looked like jungles and heavy machinery was used to clear them. GoSL, through funds from ENREP project, amounting to a considerable investment, brought 140,000 acres under paddy cultivation.

**Distribution of Agro Machinery, equipment and tools in the resettled areas**

| Items | 2009 | | | | | 2010 | | | | | 2011 | | Total |
|---|---|---|---|---|---|---|---|---|---|---|---|---|---|
| | Jaffna | Kilinochchi | Mullaitivu | Vavuniya | Mannar | Jaffna | Kilinochchi | Mullaitivu | Vavuniya | Mannar | Kilinochchi | Mullaitivu | |
| 4w Tractor | 1 | 10 | 10 | 5 | 11 | 122 | 132 | 134 | 69 | 100 | | | 594 |
| 2w Tractor | 25 | 20 | 20 | 15 | 20 | 35 | 200 | 186 | 85 | 136 | | | 742 |
| Water Pumps | 230 | 210 | 95 | 5 | 258 | 33 | 864 | 1,145 | 726 | 239 | 2,200 | 2,200 | 9,438 |
| Knapsack Sprayer | 18 | 205 | 98 | 100 | 12 | 67 | 371 | 383 | 300 | 245 | | | 1,799 |
| Power Sprayer | | | | | 20 | 6 | 2 | 2 | 5 | 5 | | | 40 |

Source: Department of Agriculture

Major contribution was received from GoI, as a result of intervention by His Excellency the President during his visit to India in 2010. INGOs / NGOs were directed to support this endeavour.

**Provision of Seed Paddy**

| District | Seed paddy distributed (KG) | Extent benefited (Acres) | Number of farmers benefited | Own seed paddy used |
|---|---|---|---|---|
| Jaffna | 3824 | 962 | 733 | |
| Killinochchi | 122932 | 40977 | 17133 | 22583 |
| Mullaitivu | 73645 | 24512 | 9065 | |
| Vavuniya | 55831 | 18580 | 6900 | |
| Mannar | 64371 | 21457 | 10259 | |
| **Total** | 320603 | 106488 | 44090 | 22583 |

Source: Department of Agriculture

Provision of seed paddy and distribution was well planned. In this regard, FAO and Department of Agriculture performed an excellent work to encourage farmers by providing seed paddy in time. That was a major achievement. In addition to the supply of seed paddy, provision of subsidy fertilizers, for all cultivation seasons, after resettlement and provision of agriculture machinery, in time, contributed immensely to revival of agriculture.

**Provision of subsidised fertilizers issued by GoSL**

| Season | Quantity issued in MT | | |
|---|---|---|---|
| | MOP | Urea | TSP |
| 2009 / 10 Maha | 1811.877 | 7084.757 | 2140.357 |
| 2010 Yala | 300.959 | 1537.113 | 474.709 |
| 2010 / 11 Maha | 4370.028 | 15557.594 | 5052.483 |
| 2011 Yala | 148.587 | 515.399 | 187.766 |

Source: Ministry of Agriculture - Northern Province

It must be noted that fertilizer was made available immediately after resettlement, to enable them to quickly recommence their main livelihood in immediate Maha season (2009/10) and followed by the next season (2010/ 11). Value of fertilizer provided for all the seasons referred to above is Rs. 1,548.07 million.

**Cultivation of Abandoned paddy land from Years 2009 to 2011**

| District | Cultivable Extent (Ac) | Total abandoned paddy land on 2009 (Ac) | Achievement Extent (Ac) | | | | |
|---|---|---|---|---|---|---|---|
| | | | Maha 2009/-2010 | Yala 2010 | Maha 2010/-2011 | Yala 2011 | Balance |
| Jaffna | 32,361 | 8,394 | 2,000 | 0 | 962 | 0 | 5,432 |
| Vavuniya | 52,540 | 22,999 | 3,653 | 306 | 18,580 | 65 | 460 |
| Mannar | 57,710 | 44,805 | 12,750 | 1,100 | 21,457 | 750 | 9,498 |
| Mullaitivu | 41,340 | 41,340 | 2,900 | 2,800 | 18,316 | 1,5-14 | 16,828 |
| Kilinochchi | 63,454 | 63,454 | 2,500 | 3,670 | 47,970 | 0 | 9,314 |
| Total | 247,405 | 180,992 | 23,803 | 7,876 | 107,2-85 | 2,3-29 | 41,532 |

Source: Dept. of Agriculture

These figures show a remarkable achievement in bringing a large extent of abandoned cultivable land under paddy cultivation.

**Paddy Production Maha 2009/10**

| District | Total Cultivated Extent (ac) | Production (Mt) |
|---|---|---|
| Jaffna | 25,967 | 34,796 |
| Kilinochchi | 6,170 | 8,453 |
| Mannar | 29,836 | 48,334 |
| Mullaitivu | 5,700 | 7,581 |
| Vavuniya | 31,500 | 44,415 |
| Total | 99,173 | 143,579 |

Source: Dept of Agriculture

**Paddy Production Maha 2010/11**

| District | Total Cultivated Extent (ac) | Production (Mt) |
|---|---|---|
| Jaffna | 25,984 | 24,699 |
| Kilinochchi | 54,140 | 49,823 |
| Mannar | 45,251 | 61,005 |
| Mullaitivu | 24,016 | 21,091 |
| Vavuniya | 43,811 | 56,104 |
| Total | 193,202 | 212,722 |

These figures reflect a success story of well-planned efforts of the GoSL in its endeavour to help the resettled communities to be engaged in their main source of income.

## Reconstruction of Irrigation System

Northern Province is largely an agricultural region in the dry zone of Sri

Lanka, having both rain-fed and irrigation farming. There are 2,000 irrigation tanks of major, medium and minor in the five districts of the Northern Province. The Government of Sri Lanka paid serious attention and drew up plans to get the system rehabilitated after the conflict to keep people engaged in agriculture. There are about 189,000 acres of land under irrigated agriculture in the Northern Province. This consists of schemes under central and provincial administration and minor irrigation schemes under Agrarian Services Development Department. Paddy cultivation has been done in four seasons since resettlement began, mainly due to rehabilitation of irrigation facilities that have been carried out during the 180-Day program.

**Details of Reservoirs under major, medium and minor irrigation schemes**

|  | Central Government | Provincial Council | Minor Agrarian Development Department |
|---|---|---|---|
| Number of Schemes | 9 | 54 | 176 |
| Command Area (Ac) | 38,667 | 64,665 | 80,678 |
| Cultivated in 2010/2011 Maha (Ac) | 36,650 | 42,505 | 77,700 |
| Reconstruction Investment-Allocation up to end 2011 (Rs. Mn) | 712.5 | 1,629.3 | 1,546.0 |
| Expenditure up to July 2011 (Rs. Mn) | 537.0 | 406.0 | 373.79 |

Source: Dept of Agriculture

The total commitment of the Government for restoration of the entire irrigation system including major, medium and minor tanks and irrigation network amounts to Rs. 6,333.9 million, of which Rs. 3,887.8 million was to be utilised by the end of 2011. The funds for this investment have been allocated from the five projects implemented by the GoSL, in the Northern Province.

## Fisheries Sector

Fishery is the second most important work activity, following agriculture in the Northern Province. Almost one third of the coastal line is in the Northern Province and annual average production of fish had been recorded at 75,000 metric tons. The coastal fisheries have experienced wide spread destruction of production assets including boats, fishing gear and serious damages to supporting infrastructure, such as harbours, boat-yards, production facilities, ice plants and fuel supply stations. Multiple displacements and restriction of fishing areas due to security concerns also affected the fishing industry. By the year 2008, annual production was reduced to 15,000 metric tons. In response to community needs, the Government provided fishing gear and other equipment for sea, lagoon and inland fishing, under the 180-Day program. At the initial stage, Sri Lanka Army repaired approximately 70 boats and the Ministry of Fisheries carried out an extensive work, by providing initial assistance to purchase fishing gear and to organise the District Offices of the Fisheries Department, to ensure efficient delivery of services, provided both by Government and other agencies.

There are 12 ongoing projects at present with a total estimated cost of Rs. 177.8 million required to establish a National Aquatic Resources Regional Centre at Poonegary. In addition, there is a special project with the assistance of the Government of India, at the cost of Rs. 39 million, to provide fishing boats and equipment to nearly 230 families in Mannar.

The assistance given for revival of fisheries sector includes the following:

| Indicators | Govt | NGO/INGO/UN | Total | Completed |
|---|---|---|---|---|
| Boats, Vallam etc | 696 | 566 | 1,262 | 1,172 |
| Fishing Gear | 2,264 | 5,098 | 7,362 | 6,751 |
| Motor Engine | 101 | 352 | 453 | 327 |

Source: Department of Fisheries

## Inland and Lagoon Fishing

Provision of inland fishing implements, such as Oru, Nets, Boats and Engines, bicycles with Fish Boxes by the GoSL was made at a cost of Rs. 38.19 million. There is a facilitation of stocking of finger links, fresh water prawns and brackish water prawns in lagoons, including famous Nandikadal at a cost of Rs. 1.43 million. Investment is made in promoting sea cucumber, oyster, lobster cultures, etc at the cost of Rs. 10.29 million.

## Livestock

The Northern Province occupied a prominent position in livestock production and contributed more than 20 per cent of the overall production in the country. About 50 – 60 per cent of the people in the Northern Province were involved in livestock rearing, poultry and goat and cattle farming, before the onset of the conflict and performing well with sufficient livestock production and effective marketing network for milk, meat and eggs. However, the conflict had a severe impact on the displaced communities where families had to completely abandon their livestock and face a total loss of their livestock assets as a result.

A concerted effort was made by the Ministry of Livestock and Rural Community Development, Department of Animal Production and the Northern Provincial Council to resuscitate the livestock sector with special attention to develop cattle farming, poultry and goat rearing.

There were no other livestock resources available at the start of resettlement, except the herds of strayed cattle grazing all over the province. An extensive program to round up the strayed cattle, vaccinate them and return them to their original owners was initiated, with the support of the Armed Forces. Nearly, 60,000 strayed cattle have been rounded up and handed over to the community.

| Credit Line | No. of Beneficiaries | Amount of Loan granted Rs. Mn |
|---|---|---|
| Sarusara - Short term agriculture | 15,496 | 1,249 |
| Awakening North | 13,979 | 1,840 |
| Prabodini | 5,016 | 258 |
| ALDL | 592 | 171 |
| Provincial Development | 639 | 886 |
| Saubagya | 115 | 210 |
| Total | 35,837 | 4,614 |

In the year 2010 and the first part of year 2011, the aim of the Government to support rural base producers of chicks, in order to boost poultry numbers and the restocking of poultry in the Province, is providing a scaling up of alternative income channelling activities, empowering and providing income to vulnerable households. Interventions aimed at genetic upgrading of breeds, addressing the issues of low productivity of traditional breeds of cattle, goat, buffalos and poultry are in operation. Assistance has been increased to strengthen the institutional capacity of livestock service producers.

## Contribution of the Banking Sector

An excellent contribution has been made by banking and non-banking sectors with the guidance and active involvement of Central Bank of Sri Lanka (CBSL). Already 20 banks have opened up their branches in the Northern Province. The CBSL took several initiatives to expand the banking and other financial facilities in the Northern Province, to facilitate the resumption of economic activities that were adversely affected by the long drawn conflict and to boost livelihood development. The CBSL designed a special refinance credit program, titled "Awakening North under Uthuru Vasannthaya" exclusively for meeting financial requirements of the conflict affected business in the province. At the same time, the CBSL encouraged and facilitated setting up of a large number of branches by both state owned banks and private banks, to ensure widespread access to financial services in the Province. In addition, approval was also given for several non-bank financial institutions to establish branches, to expand the range of financial services. The CBSL established a provincial office in Jaffna to facilitate credit schemes, operated by financial institutions.

## Disbursement of Development Credit under different credit lines implemented by the CBSL in the Northern Province

### Disbursement of Credit for different purposes 2009 - May 2011

| Purpose | No. of Loans granted | Value of Loans granted Rs. Mn |
|---|---|---|
| Agriculture - short term | 15,496 | 1,249 |
| Agriculture - long term | 7,437 | 1,327 |
| Livestock | 2,120 | 521 |
| SMEs | 5,351 | 948 |
| Fisheries | 417 | 311 |
| Micro Credit | 5,016 | 258 |
| **Total** | 35,837 | 4,614 |

Source: Ministry of Finance and Planning

### Banks that are in operation

| | |
|---|---|
| Bank of Ceylon | DFCC Vardhana Bank Ltd |
| People's Bank | Sri Lanka Savings Bank |
| National Savings Bank | Sanasa Development Bank |
| Pan Asia Bank | Sampath Bank |
| Lankaputhra Development Bank | Seylan Bank |
| Indian Bank | HSBC |
| Pradeshiya Sanwardana Bank | Nations' Trust Bank |
| MCB Bank | Hatton National Bank |
| Indian Overseas Bank | Commercial Bank |
| Housing Development Financing Corporation (HDFC) | State Mortgage and Development Bank |

## Connectivity

**Highways:** All classes of roads were completely neglected and the GoSL embarked upon a heavy investment, for restoration of the road network in the Northern Province. This includes major roads, provincial and rural access roads. In order to strengthen connectivity, heavy investment was made by the Government, to reconstruct major road networks with assistance from the Government of People's Republic of China. The details are as follows:

**Work already commenced**

| Road Name and No. | Length Km |
|---|---|
| (01) Kandy - Jaffna (A009) (Galkulama to 230 Km) | 63 |
| (02) Kandy -Jaffna (A009) (230 Km to 320 Km Jaffna) | 90 |
| Navathkuli - Karativu - Mannar (A032) | 67 |
| Puttlam - Marichikade - Mannar | 113 |
| (01) Jaffna - Point Pedro (AB020) (02) Puttur - Meesalai (AB 32) (03) Jaffna - Kankasanturai (AB 016) (04) Jaffna - Palali (AB 018) | 84 |
| (01) Mullaitivu - Kokkiilai - Pulmuddai (B297) | 42.4 |
| (02) Oddusudan - Nedunkerny (B334) | 52.6 |
| **Total Cost** | 512 |

Source: Ministry of Finance and Planning

The work has already begun. In addition, several rural roads have been repaired and restored under the 180-Day Program and by using the Government owned projects operating in the Northern Province i.e. NRCP, CARE.

The restoration of provincial roads were also commenced with the assistance of Northern Provincial Council through the Road Development

Board and the following projects are ongoing for improvement of road, infrastructure, providing access to social centres, etc. in the Northern Province.

| Name of the Project | Funded by | Project Areas | Loan Amount (US$ Mn) | Provincial Compone- nt (US$ Mn) | Date of Comme- ncement | Date of Completion |
|---|---|---|---|---|---|---|
| NRCP | GoSL & ADB Loan | Vavuniya, Mannar | 173.00 | 21.37 | June 2010 | June 2015 |
| CARE | GoSL & ADB Loan | Jaffna, Kilinochchi, Mullaitivu, Vavuniya, Mannar | 168.24 | 37.14 | June 2010 | June 2013 |
| PRP | World Bank Loan | Jaffna | 105.00 | 21.00 | March 2010 | March 2015 |

Source: Ministry of Finance and Planning

In addition, the GoSL had initiated action in the year 2010, to develop major road networks and the railway lines in the Northern Province. Loan Agreements have already been signed for both projects, contracts have been awarded and commissioning of the work in both projects commenced in year 2010 and work has continued well beyond 2011. The investment made by the GoSL for infrastructure development in the Northern Province, during the one and half years, is ample testimony to the commitment of the GoSL towards re-construction of the Northern Province.

## Railway

The entire railway network of the Northern Province was destroyed by the LTTE. Most of the railway lines and the sleepers had been taken away by the LTTE to put up bunkers. Hence, reconstruction of the railway lines is a massive commitment undertaken by the Government to support the rebuilding of the Northern Province, since the Northern railway is considered as being the live wire for the Northern people. Restoration of railway lines has commenced with a loan obtained from the Government of India.

| Package No. | Road Name | Length Km |
|---|---|---|
| 1 | Kankasanthurai to Pallai | 56 |
| 2 | Omanthai to Pallali | 90 |
| 3 | (a) Medawachchiya to Madhu | 43 |
| 4 | (b) Madhu to Tallai Mannar | 63 |
| 5 | Signalling & Telecom System | |
| | **Total** | 252 |

Source: Ministry of Finance and Planning

Work of these railway lines has already commenced.

## Bridges (Flagship Intervention)

The following bridges were completely destroyed by the LTTE, to prevent access to the Security Forces:

**Sangupiddy Bridge:** Sangupiddy Bridge was destroyed by a massive land mine in 1983. This bridge links Jaffna to Mannar, through Punerine (A32). Consequent to the defeat of the LTTE, the bridge was reconstructed at a cost of Rs. 983 million. It was declared open by H E the President on 16.01.2011, as a gift to the Northern people on Thaipongal Day. Consequent to the opening of the Bridge, the travel time from Mannar to Jaffna was reduced by 2 ½ hours and also 112 Km less than taking the A9 road via Kilinochchi to Jaffna.

**Mannar Bridge and Causeway:** Mannar Bridge was damaged due to a bomb blast by the LTTE in 1990. The new bridge, spanning 157.1 meters in length and 10.4 meters in width, was constructed with two lanes and a side walk at a cost of Rs.2.46 billion. 50,000 people living in Mannar Island directly benefit by this development. This bridge provides connectivity to

Mannar Island, with the mainland giving faster and safer access to the public. Mannar Bridge was opened by H.E. the President on 18.03.2011.

**Aruvi Aru Bridge at Arippu in Mannar District:** The LTTE blasted the bridge at Arippu in 1991. The public had no access and had to use a boat service to cross the river. The reconstructed bridge, spanning 251 meters in length and 7.35 meters in width, was opened on 08.12.2010. This is the longest bridge in the liberated area of Vanni, costing Rs. 151.4 million.

## Communication

## Reconstruction of Kokkavil Multifunctional Self-standing Transmission Tower

The tower built in 1982 was destroyed by the LTTE and as a result, the people in the North had no radio, television or internet facilities. The tallest and largest self-standing transmission tower (170 meters) in South Asia was reconstructed at the cost of Rs. 330 million. The construction of a multifunctional communication tower is an important mile post on the road to achieving the cherished objective of Sri Lanka, that is to be a Regional Hub for Asian Telecommunication Network.

## Re-establishment of Local Government Process

Local Authorities elections in the Northern Province were not held since 1990. The right of franchise for people living in the Northern Province has been restored. The people had the freedom for the first time to elect people of their choice. The GoSL acted expeditiously to enable provincial Council elections to take place in the Eastern Province, shortly after the East was liberated. The elections of local authorities in the Northern Province were held on 23rd July, 2011 in 33 Pradeshiya Sabhas, in all 5 districts of the Northern Province and 375 members were elected for the first time in decades. The people, in the areas previously dominated by the LTTE, had the opportunity to participate in the democratic process, without duress.

The prospering of political plurality in these areas can be seen by the triumph of the opposition party that emerged triumphant in the North where as the main Government Party emerged triumphant in the East and came second in the North, during the General Elections held in 2010.

## Conclusion

The reconstruction of the Northern Province after more than three decades of destruction is indeed a challenging task. The Northern Province has just emerged from devastation with the hope of transforming into a region of hope and rejuvenation. The GoSL has observed that the people in the Northern Province are satisfied with the achievements of the ongoing efforts for reconstruction of the Northern Province. The present reconstruction program, initiated by the Government, has been discussed at the international forums as well. It is a discernible factor that there had been no negative criticism of the ongoing resettlement and development program in any one of these forums. Even the visiting diplomats have accepted that there is a vast improvement in the region. Sri Lanka, despite many challenges, is in the process of chartering a new course to transform the Northern region, from conflict to stability. The efforts of the Government for rebuilding the North are based on the principles embodied in the "***Mahinda Chinthanaya***", the overall policy of the President of Sri Lanka. "Mahinda Chinthanaya" refers to an integrated society consisting of ***one country – one law***. The program for the Northern development is driven by this concept.

# Challenges of Harmonising
# Ethnic Diversity

# Ethnicity and Nation Building: Lessons from South Asia and Beyond

## 9

### N. Manoharan

"We have made Italy; now we must make Italians," remarked Maasimo d'Azeglu, an Italian statesman, soon after Italy's unification in the 19th Century.[1] Most of the states in South Asia had to undergo similar style of nation building after decolonisation in the middle of the 20th century. Even after six decades since their birth, the painful process is still on. Nation building indeed is not an outcome, but a continuous process. Rome was not built in a day. The multi-ethnic nature of states of South Asia has made the nation building process problematic. However, it would be utterly wrong to conclude that ethnicity is the main hurdle in nation building, though it may be one of the faultlines.

Statistically speaking, of about 200 states, only 12 (nine per cent) could justifiably be called nation states in the sense that the boundaries of the "territorial-juridical entity being coterminous or approximately coterminous with the distribution of a particular national group." Yet, not all are facing ethnic secessionism.[2] Also, not all ethnic groups are secessionists. The Indian

---

[1] Quoted in Charles L. Killinger, *History of Italy* (Westport: Greenwood Publishing Group, 2002), p. 1.

[2] According to *SIPRI Yearbook* (2011), in 2010, 15 major armed conflicts were active in 15 locations around the world. Of these, only four of the major armed conflicts in 2010 were over territory, while 11 were being fought over the government. Over the decade of 2001–10, only 2 of the total of 29 major armed conflicts have been interstate.

case suggests that too much of diversity is also an advantage, where it is difficult to mobilise a critical mass against the state. For instance, lack of a dominant ethnic group in India also made accommodation easier to achieve. The process of nation building, therefore, has to be looked at in a comprehensive manner. While accepting that every state is different and so is the nation building process, the chapter argues that one can always draw lessons (or ideas at the least) from different cases. The attempt here is to do exactly that. Asian and African cases are given more emphasis due to their relevance and the wide ranging lessons that they offer.

## Ethnicity and Nation building: In Context

The political importance of 'ethnicity' has gained currency particularly since the Second World War, defying predictions of early twentieth century social theorists that 'ethnicity' and 'nationalism' would lose their importance in the wake of modernisation, industrialisation and individualism. This made Ronald Cohen remark, "quite suddenly, with little comment or ceremony, ethnicity is ubiquitous."[3] Birth of numerous states with the demise of colonialism and the subsequent assertion of self-determination, based on ethnicity and the continuous influx of migrants and refugees to the developed countries, were the major reasons for ethnicity remaining in the forefront of the international agenda of sovereign states.[4]

To Nathan Glazer and Daniel Moynihan, "ethnicity seems to be a new term."[5] Though its first usage is attributed to American sociologist David Riesman,[6] its root, 'ethnos', is archaic enough to be mentioned by ancient Greeks to mean 'heathen' or 'pagan'. The dictionary entries generally give the meaning for the word 'ethnic' as "of involving a nation, race or tribe

---

[3] Ronald Cohen, "Ethnicity: Problem and Focus in Anthropology," *Annual Review of Anthropology*, Vol. 7, 1978, p. 379.

[4] Thomas Hylland Eriksen, *Ethnicity and Nationalism: Anthropological Perspectives* (London: Pluto Press, 1993), p. 12.

[5] Nathan Glazer and Daniel P. Moynihan, "Introduction," in Nathan Glazer and Daniel P. Moynihan (eds.), *Ethnicity: Theory and Experience* (Cambridge: Harvard University Press, 1975), p. 1.

[6] It came into being in the context of a debate on McCarthyism, loyalty, and intellectual freedom. See David Riesman, "Some Observations on Intellectual Freedom," *American Scholar*, Vol. 23, No. 1, Winter 1953-54, pp. 9-25.

that has a common cultural tradition." The terms 'ethnic' and 'ethnicity' are used here to include religious, racial, linguistic, tribal and similar divides which have been activated in socio-political conflicts in the present age. Thus, ethnicity is a concept referring to a shared culture and way of life, especially as reflected in language, folkways, religious and other institutional forms, material culture such as clothing and food and cultural products such as music, literature, and art. The use of the single generic term is justified by the palpable fact that the common features of these conflicts greatly overshadow the specificity of their religious, racial, linguistic or tribal character.[7]

'Essentialists' or 'Primordialists'[8] argue that collective ethnic identities are deeply rooted historical continuities nurtured by early socialisation and reinforced by collective sanctions. Its basic assumption is that ethnic conflicts of today between the groups can be traced back to older animosities. Such animosities are based on inherent ethnic differences. These intrinsic group differences activate prejudices and trigger violence over and again defying rationality. To 'Instrumentalists',[9] ethnic identities and solidarities are fluid, pragmatic and opportunistic often constructed by ethnic entrepreneurs, irrespective of their belief in ethnicity, to justify demands for political and especially material advantages. In other words, ethnicity is strategically manipulated by the elite for the sake of power, irrespective of their belief in the ethnic categories. Thus, they create cleavages or build bridges according to the gains or losses from such manipulation.

---

[7] Glazer and Moynihan, n. 5, pp. 7-10.

[8] Includes Clifford Geertz, *The Interpretation of Cultures* (New York: Basic, 1973); and Walker Connor, *Ethnonationalism* (Princeton: Princeton University Press, 1994).

[9] Russell Hardin, *One for All: The Logic of Group Conflict* (Princeton: Princeton University Press, 1995); Ronald Rogowski, "Causes and Varieties of Nationalism: A Rationalist Account," in R. Rogowski and E. Teriyakia, *New Nationalism of the Developed West* (London: Routledge, 1985); Michael Hechter, "Explaining Nationalist Violence," *Nations and Nationalism*, Vol. 1, No. 1, April 1995; Paul Brass, *Language, Religion and Politics in North India* (Cambridge: Cambridge University Press, 1973) (who is now a postmodernist) and to some extent, Ernest Gellner, *Nations and Nationalism* (Oxford: Oxford University Press), 1983.

According to 'Institutionalists',[10] ethnic identities were constructed in recent history and ethnicity is a modern phenomenon. To them, in earlier days, identities operated on a small scale and were flexible. Conflicts were managed locally and were not taken at the identity level. But, in modern times, with development of printing press and capitalism, the identities got wider and institutionalised. Thus, even individual conflicts can be blown up into a larger conflict by interested groups or elites by constructing a "master narrative". Ethnic identities are linked to the political system and the institutions in a particular country. Ethnically plural countries require different type of institutions from that of mono-ethnic societies. Thus, an unexamined transference of political systems or institutional forms of governance, regardless of ethnic categories in a particular society, can be a serious cause for ethnic conflict. At the same time, a careful institutional choice would mitigate conflicts.

However, the common thread which runs in all the above theoretical arguments is that ethnicity has something to do with the classification of people and group relationships. Ethnicity is thus "an aspect of social relationship between agents who consider themselves as being culturally distinctive from members of other groups with whom they have a minimum of regular interaction."[11] It has a reference group in relation to which a sense of 'relative deprivation' is aggregated and aggravated. In other words, ethnicity is fundamentally a self ascribed phenomenon, though it is influenced by how cultural difference is delineated by others.

'Nation building' refers to the process of constructing a national identity by remoulding different groups into a single nation. This process aims at the unification of the people within the state so that it remains politically stable and viable in the long-run. It is the "most common form of a process of collective identity formation with a view to legitimising public power

---

[10] Eric Hobsbawm and Terence Ranger, *The Invention of Tradition* (Cambridge: Cambridge University Press, 1983); Linda Cooley, *Britons: Forging the Nation, 1707-1837* (New Haven: Yale University Press, 1983); Benedict Anderson, *Imagined Communities* (London: Verso, 1983).

[11] Eriksen, n. 4, p. 14.

within a given territory."[12] Nation building can involve the use of propaganda or major infrastructure development to foster social harmony and economic growth. It involves deliberate manipulation of identities at a different level in which the State plays the key role. For this purpose, there is a need to create national paraphernalia such as the national flag, anthem, emblem, day, language, history, legacy, myth, edifices and various other shared symbols. To Antony Smith, "ceremonies, symbols and myths are crucial to nationalism, through them nations are formed and celebrated."[13] Singling out 'national history', one scholar pertinently observes, "for individuals to be able to cultivate national feelings, it is important that the story the nation tells itself about its past should be generally believed, but need not be historically accurate."[14] Jean-François Lyotard characterises this as a "great narrative." To Riggs, this is "state nationalism" where a state creates a nation, manufactures and nourishes imagery, and communicates a package of ideals.[15]

Nation building, thus, is a question of creating absolute loyalty, a sense of belonging, patriotism to the country one belongs to. It is a large concept including the development of all the aspects of political, socio-cultural, military and economic systems of a society. The linkage of a nation to a state embodies successful nationalist mobilisation. In these cases, nationalist symbols, institutions and rhetoric have been identified with and internalised to such an extent that they constitute common sense, the ultimate goal of any movement pursuing a nationalist project.[16] Nation-building describes the nationalist project of states which aim to hold on to their conceptual

---

[12] Armin von Bogdandy et al, "State-Building, Nation-Building and Constitutional Politics in Post-Conflict Situations: Conceptual Clarifications and an Appraisal of Different Approaches," in A. von Bogdandy and R. Wolfru, (eds.), *Max Planck Yearbook of United Nations Law,* Vol. 9, 2005, p. 579-613.

[13] Anthony D. Smith, *Nations and Nationalism in a Global Era* (Cambridge: Polity Press, 1996), p. 150.

[14] Yael Tamir. "The Enigma of Nationalism," *World Politics*, Vol. 47, No. 3, April 1995, pp. 418-40.

[15] F. W. Riggs, "Modernity and Bureaucracy," *Public Administration Review*, Vol. 57, No. 4, 1997, p. 351.

[16] Claire Sutherland, "Nation-building through discourse theory," *Nations and Nationalism*, Vol. 11, No. 2, 2005, p. 193.

hegemony over the nodal point – 'nation'.[17] The term 'nation-building' covers not only conscious strategies initiated by state leaders, but also un-planned societal changes. It is the building of that common identity what Benedict Anderson called as "imagined community".[18]

State-building' is but one component of nation-building, albeit an integral component. It involves the creation and development of the institutions of a political system. Although in phases, nation and state building in Europe went on for several centuries.[19] But, in that sense, most of the South Asian countries are very young nations – not even a century old. While in Europe nation-building historically preceded state-building, in post colonial states, state building preceded nation building. The newly independent developing states were characterised by "their colonial background, the arbitrary construction of their boundaries by external powers, the lack of societal cohesion, their recent emergence into juridical statehood, and their stage of development."[20] They inherently had anxieties over threats to their security, unity, sovereignty and territorial integrity. Therefore, protecting these 'core values' became the priority. In other words, state rather than nation-building was given utmost primacy.

---

[17] W. Connor, *Ethnonationalism – The Quest for Understanding* (Princeton, NJ: Princeton University Press, 1994), p. 40.

[18] See Benedict Anderson, *Imagined Communities* (London: Verso, 1994).

[19] Stein Rokkan's model saw nation-building as consisting of four analytically distinct aspects. In Western Europe, these as-pects had usually followed each other in more or less the same order. Thus, they could be regarded not only as aspects but also as *phases* of nation-building. The first phase resulted in economic and cultural unification at the elite level. The second phase brought ever larger sectors of the masses into the system through conscription into the army, enrollment in compulsory schools, etc. The burgeoning mass media created channels for direct contact between the central elites and periphery populations and generated widespread feelings of identity with the political system at large. In the third phase, the subject masses were brought into active participation in the workings of the territorial political system. Finally, in the last stage, the administrative apparatus of the state expanded. Public welfare services were established and nation-wide policies for the equalisation of economic conditions were designed.

[20] Mohammed Ayoob, "State Making, State Breaking and State Failure: Explaining the Roots of Third World Insecurity," Paper prepared for the seminar on 'Conflict and Development: Causes, Effects and Remedies,' The Hague, Netherlands Institute of International Relations, 22-24 March 1994, pp. 2-3.

This does not mean that nation building was totally disregarded. However, in many newly independent states, the ruling elite tried to build the nation on the basis of the language or religion of the majority community, to the exclusion of sentiments and identities of minorities. In response, the alienated minority groups initially demanded sufficient autonomy, basically through non-violent means, to safeguard their identities from assimilationist tendencies of the majoritarian state. But, when their demands were put down with force, they manifested into secessionism that was, at times, termed as 'national revolution'. For this, secessionist movements needed to emphasise cultural markers in their definition of the nation more than autonomist movements.[21] In Sri Lanka, for example, when the political system gravitated from consensual politics to competitive politics to conflictual politics and then to confrontational politics, Tamil identity gradually gained momentum developing a separate concept of 'Eelam'.

Whenever there is an element of domination or lack of accommodation in any nation building exercise, challenges from "peripheral nationalism" come to the fore. Sub-state challenges to the constitutional status quo use the same ideological principles, but adapt them to an alternative national construct. They attempt to break the link embodied in the term 'nation-state' by bringing about a 'crisis of the hyphen'.[22] The approach of the majoritarian governments was to view minority agitation as a law and order problem. Gradually the insurgencies got entrenched; a war of attrition ensued, posing a challenge to the stability and security of the state. The insurgent groups tried to get legitimacy by mobilising international support that includes not only state actors, but also those from the diaspora. Interestingly, some of them, like the Tamils in Sri Lanka and the Bengalis in East Pakistan, received sustenance from kinsmen across the borders. In order to sustain the struggle, many insurgent groups did not hesitate to resort to terrorism as a means.

---

[21] André Lecours, "Ethnic and Civic Nationalism: Towards a New Dimension," *Space and Polity*, Vol. 4, Issue 2, 2000, pp. 153-66.

[22] Cited in D. McCrone, *The Sociology of Nationalism* (London: Routledge, 1998), p. 173.

## Lessons: From South Asia and Beyond

The character of nation building depends, by and large, on the manner in which a new state is born. It could be after the end of a violent conflict by victory or defeat of a militant group; it could be after peaceful transfer of power or negotiated settlement or through non-violent struggle. The type of institutions, nature of constitution, power sharing, form of government, etc. depend by and large, on these scenarios.

## Institutions

Most of the problems in ethnic relations arise because of failure or the biased nature of existing/old institutions. Therefore, the first and foremost requisite in the nation building process is the provision of functioning state institutions, but these are seen as fair by all communities. Those countries that are emerging from conflicts especially need better institutions just to avoid repetition of old predicaments. Generally speaking, there are two broad alternative approaches to institution building. One may be called 'Reconstruction Model', under which the idea is to work within existing institutions and to deal, more or less impartially, with all social forces and power centres, to redirect their ongoing competition for power and prosperity, from violent to peaceful channels. The alternative approach can be termed as the 'Deconstruction Model', under which authorities first dismantle an existing state apparatus and then build a new one.[23] But the problem arises when these methods are adapted to suit interests of particular communities or individuals in power.

## Constitution

Among the state institutions, the Constitution is vital. It lays down a structures of legitimate authority and also national goals that form the basic edifice on which the nation rests. A good constitution takes care of several things in a state – its structure, form of government, relations between different entities of the state, legislative procedure, rights and duties of the people and so on. Constitutions have an additional role of an instrument that can mediate identity

---

[23] The Beginner's Guide to Nation-Building, p. xx

conflicts by reconciling "sameness and difference".[24] There are two main tools in constitutional nation-building: the form and procedure of constitution making and the institutional arrangements provided in the constitution.

For the legitimacy of a new constitution, the process is as important as the content of the final document.[25] Indian and South African examples demonstrate that the inclusiveness of the constitution-making process towards a constitutional compact ("representativeness" of the Constitution making body) is decisive for the development of a common identity to underline nation-building ("sense of building constitutional institutions").[26] Habermas talks about the concept of "constitutional patriotism" where the Constitution itself can become the focal object of collective loyalties and even pushes other objects of identification to obscurity.[27] For instance, many Americans see their state and their nation as essentially coterminous and both originating from the Declaration of Independence and the 1787 Constitution.

In considering the constitutional design, the first step is to analyse the sources of violent conflict in the society. The higher the stakes of an ethnic group and its leadership in the central power structure, the greater are the possibilities of nation-building.[28] It is necessary to reassure all sections of the population about the prospects of their groups in a new constitutional arrangement. Agreement on constitutional principles within such a body, as happened in South Africa, has an immensely reassuring effect on society as a whole. By providing openings for individual and group identities to focus on the dignified parts of the Constitution, the "educational" purpose of a constitutional text created in post-conflict situations can be supported and amplified and thus help to prevent the emergence of mere "semantic constitutionalism". For this, as Thomas Cooley and Alexander Hamilton

---

[24] Lidija R. Basta Fleiner, "Constitution Making and Nation Building," available at http://www.constitutionnet.org/files/Basta-Fleiner.pdf, accessed on 10 October 2011

[25] Vivian Hart, "Democratic Constitution Making," United Stated Institution for Peace, Special Report No. 107, July 2003, p. 1.

[26] Lidija R. Basta Fleiner, "Constitution Making and Nation Building," available at http://www.constitutionnet.org/files/Basta-Fleiner.pdf, accessed on 12 October 2011.

[27] J. Habermas, *The Inclusion of the Other: Studies in Political Theory* (Cambridge, MA: MIT Press, 1998), 225

[28] Urmila Phadnis and Rajat Ganguly, *Ethnicity and Nation-building in South Asia* (New Delhi: Sage Publications, 2001), p. 14.

had stated, the task of constitution writing is essential to the building of new nations, on the basis of 'reflection and choice' rather than by 'accident and force'. It is not an exaggeration to observe that success to India's sustenance as one country is mainly due to its strong constitutional framework. Crucially, unlike some of its neighbours that witnessed many constitutions during their existence, the Indian Constitution has stood the test of time.[29]

## Form of Government

In the context of nation-building, amongst all forms of governments, democracy is seen as a practical means of redirecting the ongoing competition into peaceful channels, especially in multi-ethnic societies. Democratic systems foster compromise on the major political questions. However, it has its own ills if understood purely in electoral form. Rabushka and Shepsle argued that democracy in an ethnically plural society inevitably releases "ethnic outbidding" behaviours as politicians vie for votes in the electoral marketplace.[30] In that case, it believes in the power of numbers – empowers majorities and potentially dis-empowers minorities.[31] There is, thus, an inherent "minority problem" that must be dealt with. How does one go about it? Robert Dahl suggests that through power sharing arrangements or through systems of federal autonomy, the "minority problem" could be overcome.[32]

Andrew Reynolds observes that "parliamentarism, proportional representation, and power sharing structures provide the foundational level of inclusion, needed by precariously divided societies to pull themselves out

---

[29] A study by Ginsberg, Elkins and Blount points out that worldwide, the average lifespan of a constitution is just 17 years. See Elkins, Zachary, Tom Ginsburg, and Justin Blount, "Does the Process of Constitution-Making Matter?" *Annual Review of Law and Social Science*, Vol. 5, 2009, p. 202.

[30] See Alvin Rabushka and Kenneth Shepsle, *Politics in Plural Societies: A Theory of Democratic Instability* (Columbus, OH: Merrill, 1972).

[31] At its extreme, Estonia and Latvia followed the model of "ethnic democracy" in which the state is conceived of as belonging to the ethnic majority and is seen as a means for advancing its national interests and goals, while minorities are viewed as potentially disloyal and are not permitted fully equal citizenship rights. See Sammy Smooha, "The Model of Ethnic Democracy," ECMI Working Paper #13, European Center for Minority Issues, Flensburg, Germany, 2001.

[32] Robert Dahl, *Polyarchy: Participation and Opposition* (New Haven, CT: Yale University Press, 1971), pp. 114-18.

of the maelstrom of ethnic conflict and democratic instability."[33] Appropriate power sharing arrangements limit the authority of the majority and provide guarantees to the development of the minority communities. In divided societies, public services may contribute to the maintenance of a delicate balance between groups. Public services have had and still have, in the case of developing or post conflict countries, a role in nation and identity building and pacification.[34] Public administration, public institutions and public services may help to resolve cultural conflicts between majorities and minorities. Bourgeois speaks, in this context of "administrative consociationalism"[35]. Such processes of accommodation are especially visible in ethnically divided societies where quotas are sometimes used in the distribution of public offices. India is a classic case of such accommodation where there are multiple quotas. This affirmative action model from India may suit other countries, especially Sri Lanka, where instead of getting into controversial devolution of powers to geographical areas like provinces or districts, one can consider communities as units of devolution. On the whole, if democracy succeeds in providing a sense of people-hood, a common "we" to whom the state properly belongs, it will foster nation building.

## Electoral System & Political Parties

Adoption of a suitable type of electoral system is also important in the nation-building process. Electoral arrangements such as the first-past-the-post (FPTP) system are generally criticised for their failure to ensure a fair representation of ethnic minorities. W. Arthur Lewis goes to the extent of asserting that "the surest way to kill the idea of democracy in a plural society is to adopt the Anglo-American system of first-past-the-post."[36] But, this is

---

[33] See Andrew Reynolds, *Electoral Systems and Democratisation in Southern Africa* (New York: Oxford University Press, 1999).

[34] V. A. Thompson, "Bureaucracy in a Democratic Society," in C. M. Roscoe (ed.), *Public Adminis- tration and Democracy: Essays in Honour of Paul H. Appleby* (Syracuse: Syracuse University Press, 1965), p. 208. Also see R. J. I. Stillman, *Public Administration: Concepts and Cases* (Bos- ton: Houghton Mifflin Company), 2000), p. 18.

[35] D. Bourgeois, "Administrative Nationalism," *Administration and Society,* Vol. 39, No. 5, 2007, pp. 631-55.

[36] *Quoted in Andrew Reynolds, "Constitutional Engineering in Southern Africa,"* Journal of Democ- racy *Vol. 6, No. 2, 1995, p. 86.*

the case only if the minority communities are scattered. For instance, the FPTP system did not impact Tamils in Sri Lanka much because of their concentration in the north and the east of the island. However, when the successive Sri Lankan governments started settling Sinhalese in the east, Tamils started losing their electoral advantage. To correct it, Proportional Representation (PR) was considered a better form of electoral system to reflect on the plurality in the society. Yet, it failed to make much difference to the Tamil minorities because while introducing PR electoral system to its Parliament, the 1978 Constitution also introduced the Presidential system. PR works better in the parliamentary form of government. In general, however, the PR system is thought effective in nation building efforts, as it tends to increase voter participation and encourage political parties to seek votes and membership across communities.[37]

Nevertheless, a one-size-fits-all approach does not work. Societies are divided in different ways and in different conditions; this needs to be taken into account when considering electoral systems. For instance, despite its plural nature, the independent India preferred the FPTP system, as against proportional representation, because of its simplicity for the predominantly illiterate population at that point in time. There is no such a thing as the perfect electoral system. However, it is undeniable that some systems have advantages over the others. Care should also be taken when drawing up electoral boundaries so that ethnic or other divisions are not reinforced through homogenous constituencies.[38]

In this regard, it is also important to take into consideration the role of political parties that are in the business of 'interest articulation' and are usually accused of ethnicising conflicts in societies and profit on ethnicisation. Expecting such an eventuality of the Indian National Congress getting itself into vote bank politics after independence, Mahatma Gandhi advocated its dismantlement. But, he did not push his advocacy too hard because the

---

[37] Dennis K. Kadima, "Choosing an Electoral System: Alternatives for the Post-War Democratic Republic of Congo," Paper prepared for the Workshop on 'Electoral Perspectives and the Process of Democratisation in the DRC: Lessons from SADC Countries', Kinshasa, 21-25 October 2001.

[38] Ben Reilly, "Electoral Systems for Divided Societies," *Journal of Democracy*, Vol. 21, No. 2, April 2002, pp. 156-70.

Congress, on the positive side, served as an integrating force in the initial years. Similarly, in the South African case, the African National Congress, despite getting over two-thirds majority on its own, placed emphasis on forming a national government by giving opposition parties high and influential positions in the government. It also pushed non-racial agenda forward, disregarding electoral advantages. On the other hand, political parties in Bangladesh, Sri Lanka and Pakistan indulged in plebiscitary politics to the detriment of the nation-building process.

## Reconciliation, Accountability and Civil Nationalism

Establishing the balance between retribution and reconciliation in societies, emerging from conflict or tyranny, presents a particular challenge. Whom to punish and whom to forgive, whom to exclude from the new dispensation and whom to co-opt into it are choices that cannot be entirely avoided, these challenges are faced. It has to suit itself to the needs, aspirations and situations in a particular country. Despite facing over three centuries of apartheid and racial polarisation, South Africa chose the method of reconciliation. Prospect of a peaceful and progressive future together requires reconciliation and agreement on the events of the past, a common history and forgiveness on all sides. Truth commissions lie near the opposite end of the retribution spectrum. These are non-judicial inquiries into past abuses with a view to assessing blame but not levying penalties. In going down this route, the affected community declares, "We are prepared to forgive."

War crimes tribunals provide a judicial vehicle for holding accountable, those most responsible for past atrocities. In the context of nation-building, war crime tribunals and lustration should be employed only in those rare situations in which the intervening authorities are equipped to enforce the outcome and are ready to deal effectively with the resultant resistance. Applied in any other circumstances, the effect is likely to be an increased polarisation of the society in question and an eventual resumption of violence. This should be kept in mind, in the Sri Lankan case, by those who call for war crimes' investigation.

The local society will seldom be capable of mounting a credible legal process. International tribunals, on the other hand, are hugely expensive and may lack legitimacy in the eyes of the affected populations. Mixed tribunals, in which international and local judges sit together, can help to address some of these difficulties. Sri Lanka can consider exploring this option. It is clearly easier to exact retribution in circumstances in which the conflict has produced clear winners and losers, particularly if the losers have lost so badly as to preclude any further resistance. This is the case in Sri Lanka, but not in Nepal.

This is where 'civic nationalism' comes to play. The concept fosters loyalty to a political community, usually the nation-state and is tolerant and inclusive. It propounds an allegiance to political institutions like the Constitution and democracy and principles like common citizenship, rights and obligations rather than a particular ethnic group. 'Civic nationalism', therefore, is a critically important factor for nation-building since it fosters a shared public culture and supports meaningful participation in the activities of the state. In the Indian case, it is reflected in 'Unity in Diversity' because of the diverse nature of the country, in various ways. In South Africa, the concept is put in different terms – 'unity in adversity' – in the face of international hostility and internal black opposition.[39] The ANC's "rainbow nation"[40] approach embraces cultural diversity through the practice of "interculturalism" that recognises commonalities, reduces tensions and promotes the formation of social partnerships among different cultural groups. This is reflected in a two-pronged approach, coupling political and socio-economic transformation with the socio-psychological aspect of forging a broad and inclusive national consciousness.

## Connectivity and Economic Development

Why are ethno-nationalist movements active, generally, at the geographical periphery of a country? Take, for instance, Jammu and Kashmir, Punjab and the Northeastern region in the case of India; Chittagong Hill Tracts in Bangladesh; East Pakistan, Balochistan & Pashtunistan in Pakistan;

[39] Vasu Gounden, "Reflections on Identity Conflicts and Nation Building in Contemporary South Africa," *Peace Prints: South Asian Journal of Peacebuilding*, No. 3, Vol. 2, Winter 2010, p. 3.

[40] The term 'rainbowism' was coined by Archbishop Desmond Tutu to denote South Africa's multi-racial society and the peaceful coexistence of different identities. The Rainbow metaphor projects the image of different racial, ethnic and cultural groups being united and living in harmony.

Northeast in Sri Lanka; Terai in Nepal; Kurdistan in Turkey; Pattani region in Thailand; Basques in Spain; Northern Ireland; Quebecois in Canada; Chechnya in Russia. This is mainly because of their sense of "remoteness" from the "mainland". Ethnicity causes ethnic movements after being left out of the developmental process or even being a victim of uneven development.

Successful nation building, therefore, requires not only political commitment but also enormous economic resources.[41]

Better connectivity, good governance and development foster nation building. Networks create a visible distinction between 'in' and 'out' and help to establish clear territorial boundaries. They immensely contribute to the integration of 'peripheries', to the consolidation of a territory, to a standardisation thereby facilitating exchange, mobility and equity and may be used as a tool for power-brokering, pacification, and accommodation.[42] Eugen Weber refers to road building in France in the 19th century – dubbed as "administrative highways" – to effectively link the centre to the periphery. They acted as symbols of state presence, by facilitating the movement of troops, tax collectors, school inspectors and various other state office bearers.[43]

In the developmental approach to nation building, the concept is fashioned as investment in infrastructural projects like roads, railways, dams, electricity grids etc. in the areas which lag behind economically. It is also better to use local people instead of imported labour for reconstruction in the post conflict phase. Such an arrangement not only provides much needed livelihood for the locals, but it would also give a sense of belonging to them. This is very much applicable to the case of Afghanistan, where many external

---

[41] Minxin Pei and Sara Kasper, "Lessons from the Past: The American Record on Nation Building," Policy Brief No. 24, Carnegie Endowment for International Peace, May 2003, p. 6.

[42] Steven Van de Walle and Zoë Scott, "The Role of Public Services in State- and Nation-Building: Exploring Lessons from European History for Fragile States," The Governance and Social Development Resource Centre, July 2009, p. 9.

[43] Eugen Weber, *Peasants into Frenchmen: The Modernisation of Rural France – 1870-1914* (Stanford: Stanford University Press, 1976), p. 195.

[44] Bas Rietjens, Myriame Bollen, Masood Khalil, and Sayed Fazlullah Wahidi, "Enhancing the Footprint: Stakeholders in Afghan Reconstruction," *Parameters*, Spring 2009, pp. 23-25.

actors are involved in the reconstruction process and where there is an immense need for involving the local Afghans. Apart from aligning mutual expectations, such local involvement increases the trust and confidence of the government of the day, among the people.[44]

Good economic governance that promotes equitable and sustainable growth is the key to remedying underlying tensions in society. An inclusive growth enables a country to put conflict in the past and move forward with the main agenda of economic development. Failure to establish good economic governance after a conflict greatly limits the possibilities for making changes in the underlying social relations that led to the conflict, thereby increasing the chances of continued or renewed conflicts.[45]

## Leadership

The single most important determinant of the rise and fall of nations is the quality of its leadership. Much of state and nation building is likely to falter without visionary, capable and legitimate leaders. Some go to the extent of saying that political and bureaucratic "leadership is cause; everything else is effect".[46] Nationalist movements are quite often initiated by the social and political elites that go on to appeal to the large masses. Indian National Movement, American War of Independence and South African Anti-Apartheid Struggle were classic cases. The challenges of nation-building, especially in multi-ethnic societies, often seem so overwhelming that citizens look for a larger than life figure to deliver the country from its problems.[47] To the extent that leaders rise above their personal interests, political ambitions etc. and transcend parochial differences, they can play a critical role in unifying a country, however divided it may be.

On the other hand, if the leadership fails to take every community along in the nation-building process, it will result in the alienation of

---

[45] Stephen Lewarne and David Snelbecker, "Economic Governance in War Torn Economies: Lessons Learned from the Marshall Plan to the Reconstruction of Iraq," USAID, 02 December 2004.

[46] See Stephen Adei, *Leadership and Nation Building* (Accra: Combert Limited, 2004).

[47] Marvin G. Weinbaum, "Nation Building in Afghanistan: Impediments, Lessons, and Prospects," Prepared for a conference on 'Nation-Building: Beyond Afghanistan and Iraq,' sponsored by The School of Advanced International Studies, 13 April 2004.

marginalised groups. Taking the Sri Lankan case, Jeyaratnam Wilson aptly points out, "neither Senanayake nor any of this successors had, unlike Jawaharlal Nehru or Tunku Abdul Rahman, a wider vision on how a newly independent multi-ethnic polity should have political institutions, as in India and ways and means of accommodating ethnic minorities, as with Alliance Party in Malaysia, to ensure for some length of time, a peaceful polity."[48] Instead of following the inclusive approach, Sri Lankan leaders chose to have a "demotic state" in which ethnic majority was given importance at the expense of minorities.

In the South African case, Nelson Mandela, its first post-apartheid president, upon assuming office in April 1994, mobilised people behind a vision of a single nation, guided by common values and symbols. Archbishop Desmond Tutu, in his capacity as chairperson of the Truth and Reconciliation Commission, advocated for a just and tolerant society through the idea of "rainbowism".[49] The South African leadership, despite various challenges and temptations "stuck rigidly to the policy of a non-racial, non-sexist, democratic South Africa and acted firmly against any deviation from it."[50] The rest was history. Similarly, in countries like Singapore, Malaysia, Indonesia, and to some extent South Korea, individual leaders – Lee Kuan Yew, Mahathir Mohammed, Sukarno and General Park, respectively – guided the national transformation through the critical periods. Forging a consensus among various ethnic groups – what Arend Lijphart calls "consociationalism" – on major national issues, helped in the sustained nation-building.[51]

---

[48] A. Jeyaratnam Wilson, "Nation-Building in a Demotic State: The Failure of Political Leadership in Sri Lanka," in Amita Shastri and A. Jeyaratnam Wilson (eds.), *The Post Colonial States of South Asia: Democracy, Development and Identity* (London: Curzon Press, 2001), p. 88.

[49] Gounden, n. 39, p. 4.

[50] Interview with Mr Ahmed Kathrada, a South African political leader and a close associate of Nelson Mandela, *The Hindu*, 18 July 2011.

[51] For details, see Arend Lijphart, *The Politics of Accommodation* (Berkeley: University of California Press, 1968); and Arend Lijphart, *Democracy in Plural Societies* (New Haven: Yale University Press, 1977).

Problems in most of the Sub-Saharan African countries in the last several decades can be attributed to an important factor – leadership failure.[52]

## Sports

Sport is not only a physical activity but an area where people interact socially. It forms an "integral part of social life in all communities and are intricately linked to society and politics."[53] Sport is often referred to as the "conveyor of culture of the most accessible symbolism," which makes it possible to eliminate linguistic barriers and other obstacles to interaction. It is a pre-eminent area for intercultural exchange and communication. Sports, therefore, perfectly suits as a medium for overcoming feelings of socio-cultural unfamiliarity and 'otherness'. National sporting and cultural events provide an arena for a shared public culture. It is one of the major forces because it brings people together. One of Africa's statesmen, Kwame Nkrumah went to the extent of realising a 'united Africa' through sports. According to him, "sporting success gives dignity and pride; has a huge part to play in the life of a healthy community. It is an outlet for the energies of young people; develops individual character and teamwork; it gives enjoyment to people who, in many cases, have few facilities for recreation."[54] Sports can contribute to reconciliation, to the cultivation of a feeling of national unity.

In the South African context, Desmond Tutu observed, "it [sports] is probably breaking down barriers .... Watching black and white players as a team makes integration normal."[55] Key sports events such as the 1995 Rugby World Cup, 1996 soccer Africa Cup of Nations, 2003 Cricket World Cup, and the 2010 Soccer World Cup, have mobilised South Africans around a common cultural experience.[56] In the case of Liberia, sport has been the

---

[52] Stephen Adei, "The Role of Leadership in the Development of the Asian NICs and Lessons for Africa," 29th AAPAM Annual Roundtable Conference on 'Political and Managerial Leadership for Change and Development in Africa', Mbabane, Swaziland, 3 - 7 September 2007, p. 12.

[53] G. Jarvie and J. A. Maguire, *Sport and Leisure in Social Thought* (London and New York: Routledge, 1994), p. 2.

[54] Quoted in Andreas Mehler, "Political Discourse in Football Coverage – The Cases of Côte d'Ivoire and Ghana," German Institute of Global and Area Studies, Working Paper No. 27, August 2006, p. 13.

[55] Quoted in Marion Keim, *Nation building at Play: Sport as a Tool for Social Integration* (Oxford: Meyer & Meyer Sport (UK) Ltd, 2003), p. 183.

[56] Gounden, n. 39, p. 4.

magic that has kept the people together. Liberian sports journalist, Emmanuel Williams observed, "Every time the Liberian national team plays, the guns are silent. All warring factions put down their arms for a moment." So is the case with Rwanda, where "sport is an important means of restoring people's psychological equilibrium."[57] In South Asia, cricket is not only a popular game, but also a unifying force as in countries like India, Sri Lanka, Bangladesh and Pakistan. It is also seen as a symbol of triumph over colonial powers, who, in fact, introduced the game to the continent.

## Conclusion

Nation building is a very complex exercise. It is all the more difficult in an ethnically plural state. However, nation building in countries of Asia and Africa clearly demonstrates that the task is not problematic if the leadership is visionary, disregarding its personal interests, if there are inclusive political institutions that respect minority sentiments, if there is good and equal economic development and if the society is open, tolerant and forward-looking.

For the nation building to be successful, it is important that all forms of extremism, chauvinism, racism and isolationism must be guarded against and soundly sanctioned socially and politically. Things have to come from the bottom rather than top, otherwise it has no value. On the other hand, nation building through complete assimilation of ethnic minorities had largely failed all over the world. Very often it was counter-productive, regularly producing a backlash of ethnic revival-ism, which Walker Conner termed as "nation destroying" than "nation building".[58] Enforced solutions must be avoided if nation building is to succeed. 'Might' cannot and must not be shown to be 'right'. Examples from South Asia and beyond confirm this observation

The process of nation building requires a common idea of statehood and belonging, a perception of a common past, present and future. There

---

[57] Marc Broere and Elvis Ndubuisi Iruh, "The Pride of the Nation," in *People Building Peace: 35 Inspiring Stories from Around the World* (Utrecht, Netherlands: European Centre for Conflict Prevention, 1999).

[58] See Walker Conner, "Nation Building or Nation-Destroying?" *World Politics,*Vol. 24, No. 3, April 1972, pp. 319-55.

has to be a sense of pride and comfort in being part of a state. It involves the integration of national and international efforts, but in right proportions. Emerging states "need not remain wedded to text book model of the nation-state given to them." They have to find an "alternative mode of governance which is aligned with their own histories and contemporary needs of change."[59] The challenge of ethnicity to nation building is not restricted to developing countries, but also faced by developed nations as well. It is important to make the nation building project relevant to people not only through the creation of ever more effective and inclusive national symbols, but also through real economic and political reforms.

Collaboration, cooperation and new ways of thinking are the new rules of nation building. As Sam Pitroda pertinently observes, "information and communication technology are the new paradigms on the basis of which a 21st century nation has to be built. It brings openness, de-centralisation and democratisation and is a whole new model of nation building unlike the traditional one that was dependent on dominance, control and command."[60]

Whatever basis of nationalism was considered initially, may not last long. For instance, Pakistan's predominant element of nationalism in the initial years was Islam. But, that got a jolt by the birth of Bangladesh in 1971 whose basis was language. And Islam could not unite Afghans, where tribalism is the binding factor. Nation building, therefore, is a continuous process and not an end state. There is a rough sequence of what has to be done in the initial phases of nation building, involving the factors identified above. After that as Sachs say, there is "a lot of improvisation along the way."

---

[59] D. L. Sheth, "State, Nation and Ethnicity: Experience of Third World Countries," *Economic and Political Weekly*, vol. 24, No. 12, 25 March 1989, p. 619.

[60] Sam Pitroda, "Nation-building in the 21st Century and Challenges Faced," Lecture at Indian Institute of Management Alumni Association, Ahmedabad, 16 January 2011.

# Challenges to Harmonising Ethnic Diversity

**10**

### Gnana Moonesinghe

The war is over and the space for peace has opened up. The task of harmonising ethnic diversity is a complex process involving the implementation of several strategies, programs and structures that will facilitate the creation of trust and confidence amongst the multi-ethnic polity for unity and the development of a national identity. It will be appropriate to redefine centre – state structures and functions, equitable distribution of resources, welfare programs and social and cultural relationships. The introduction of liberal features for free thinking and dissent and participatory initiatives will be some of the biggest challenges in a centralised presidential system. It is up to us to make the peace process work for us. We have to be positive, look into the issues that detract us from peaceful cohabitation, try and correct them and keep moving on.

Mr. Sampanthan of the Tamil National Alliance has said in Parliament recently that,

- The Tamil people are willing to live as equal citizens within a united and undivided Sri Lanka.

- The government should address the core issues of the conflict and evolve a solution to bring about genuine reconciliation and harmony amongst the communities.

- The forces of brinkmanship should no longer influence the political agenda on the other side.

- The vast majority of people in the country Sinhalese, Tamils and Muslims are amenable to an acceptable and peaceful political solution.

This is the positive note on which I would like to start my chapter. My contention is that the sharp ethnic divisions and divisiveness of the 1956 ethos have toned down. People have, by and large, moved from the rigid positions of the '56 period. Making Sinhala the only official language in 1956 and Buddhism the foremost religion in the 1972 Constitution helped to build Sinhala consciousness, identity and pride as well as a majoritarian perspective that excluded and somewhat diminished the status of other constituent ethnic minorities of the country. But the reality soon struck the Sinhalese that none of these measures gave them the expected dividend for social and economic advancement or to effectively break into elitist stronghold; plum positions still eluded them as they lacked competence in English. These changes however introduced a sense of parochialism to the nation state while de-secularisation of the state removed one of the liberal features of the constitution, and raised issues of equity within the multi-religious polity. Also making Buddhism a populist base for politics and political manoeuvres gradually eroded much of the essence of Buddhism, the great qualities of compassion, of tolerance and of humility. By 1971 and later by the 90's, many amongst the majority recognised the need for an international language like English, to be competitive, within the country and globally. Consequently, the Sinhalese no longer take objection to English as a link language, with Sinhala and Tamil as the national languages. The present government has also taken steps to teach English and IT in all the schools.

Even the dress mode, the national attire that was identified as a representation of nationalism and the nationalist spirit has given place to the western mode of dress as a convenient form of attire, further encouraged by the aggressive commercialisation of the clothing industry.

In the case of the Tamil community, the leadership of the Tamil parties has, for the most part, continued with the emotive drive for language and culture and identity rights as features of Tamil solidarity. However with the defeat in the war, many Tamil people are war weary and politics weary and want to move on with their lives. The time is ripe for working out compromises.

The other minority, the Tamils of Indian origin, kept out of the conflict except for a few who were drawn in, either from the spectacular attraction of a 'liberation struggle' or for mercenary reasons. The Sri Lankan Indian Tamil leadership kept their people together facilitated by the community's preoccupation with their day to day problems for survival. Identity issues are a non–issue to them for the moment, although there is no doubt about the fact that this will emerge soon.

The Muslim minority community, (7% of the population) has always lived in harmony with the other communities in the country. Though a scattered population, they have a significant presence in all the provinces. But soon, they found that the aggressive mode of the Tamil leader of the separatist movement, Prabhakaran, left no space for cohabitation. The amity that previously existed between the Muslims and the Tamils evaporated quickly. Muslims in the East came under constant attack by the Tigers while the Muslims in the North were ordered to leave their homes within the hour. Yet it is encouraging to note that in the aftermath of the war, Muslims from the North and East want to return to their homes, to their lands and to their traditional economic activities - trade, agriculture and fishing.

A point that needs highlighting is that throughout the history, the communities have absorbed some features from different cultures and this has produced many an area of fusion and overlap. The three communities have been, even during periods of heightened conflict, interactive and helpful to one another at various levels. An illustration of this, of a poignant nature, is when the Muslims were evicted from Jaffna by the tigers and ordered to leave within an hour, they had no option but to entrust their valuables including jewelry to their Tamil neighbours and friends. The Tamils who took the responsibility for safekeeping the valuables did so, at the risk of offending the tigers, which may have, if discovered, carried the penalty of death. They not only kept the valuables but returned them safely to the owners. Willingness of the Muslims to return and make their homes in Jaffna with the Tamils speaks for the survivalist community needs that seek accommodation within the multi ethnic polity. Again, during the 1983 pogrom, many Sinhalese kept Tamil friends safely in their homes, risking their lives. There is, therefore, sufficient base to rebuild ruptured relations in an interdependent and mutually interactive nation.

There is a consensus built up among the ethnic groups to enter into meaningful dialogue on their mutual concerns for securing democratic freedoms and stakes in participatory governance. The thirty year war had a sobering effect on the people and they are anxious to see a settlement of their outstanding problems. If the political will is there, the settlement will not be long to find. However, if the leadership is still in the '56 mindset or afraid of the '56 mindset, then it is clear that they are not sufficiently attuned, to realise that the people have moved beyond them. Civil society will have to take the lead and show the way to the politicians as some are already beginning to.

## History revisited

At the outset, I would like to refer to two issues that have contributed to ethnic divisiveness; both relate to the selective misreading of available historical facts. The evidence that Sinhalese came from the north of India and Tamils from the South is given as the reason for the distinctiveness and cause for polarisation of the two communities on grounds of regions, racial origins and language. But a dispassionate reading of the Mahavamsa, points out facts to the contrary. It is common knowledge that when Vijaya was consecrated King of Sri Lanka, he sought as his bride, a princess from the royal family of Madurai, the state in the south of India. His companions too sought their wives from the noble families in Madurai. Sri Lankans are the result of such unions. Subsequently, many other races for instance, Malays and Arabs came and settled in Sri Lanka. By the sixteenth century and until independence, Ceylon was colonised by the Portuguese, the Dutch and the British. All these factors must have contributed to a further mix amongst the races. There are no purists amongst us although these facts are glossed over for political convenience.

The other issue refers to the battle between King Dutugemunu and King Elara, in which King Elara was defeated. The defeat of King Elara has been used as the permanent representation for placing Tamils in a secondary status and /or to show that the Sinhalese are the stronger of the two ethnic groups. When King Elara was killed, King Dutugemunu built a monument to honour a worthy king and ordered all who passed the monument to dismount as a mark of respect to King Elara. Such was the graciousness of the victor towards an opponent whom he considered his equal. Therefore the use of Dutugemunu as a symbol of racial animosity against the Tamils is totally misplaced and stands to diminish the stature of King Dutugemunu. These stories are taught in schools and children grow up with prejudice based on these misrepresentations. History must be taught in schools with the truthfulness that the subject demands. These facts are placed on record to clear the misperceptions about ethnic distortions and to eradicate ethnocentrism and intolerance.

## Understanding the complex ethnic conflict

- There are various areas where clarifications are required to understand the complex nature of the conflict. For one, there is a presumption that post war scenario presents two permanently polarised people, the majority and the minorities, the victors and the vanquished. On the contrary, the majority community and the minorities are the winners in the war against the LTTE. The distinction must be drawn between the Tigers who challenged the state and the ordinary Tamils who were the victims. If this is understood, much of the apprehensions of the government to power sharing, a preliminary step in the reconciliation process, can be assuaged.

- Peace building in an interdependent society is essentially an inclusive process involving people from different sectors, engaged in exchange of different viewpoints. Differences must be expressed without inhibitions or resentment. The people working on reconciliation should be committed to work together and continue in their efforts until a feasible plan can be worked out. At the first intimation of a stalemate, differences should not be aired in the public domain, as is often done, which is invariably detrimental to the peace building process.

- The management of the peace process in a plural society needs strong and inspired leadership that can rise above divisiveness; that can abandon ill-conceived perceptions of majoritarian supremacy; that can create a vision for the multi ethnic polity to bring in peace, trust, and human development; that can build institutions insulated for impartial and dispassionate approach to the plural polity; that believes in the Constitution, the supreme law of the land, to abide by the letter and the spirit of the laws and not be tempted to bend, distort or amend as and when the exigencies of power politics demand such manipulation.

• To hold a multi ethnic polity together, there is a need to create symbols of national identity and of ownership, to give people a sense of belonging. The national anthem, in whatever language it is sung, the flag, and the positive aspects in national achievement can be some of the vital unifying symbols.

## Tamil Leadership

There is still no unity amongst the government supported Tamil parties, the individual Tamils co-opted by the government and the other traditional Tamil parties. They do not speak with one voice about their politico-socio-economic concerns. Intra party differences are frequently aired over the media, weakening the minority cause. Success in negotiations requires formulation of new strategies for compromise and not the reassertion of the pre- war agenda. The urgent call of the people from the North and East is for basic needs and improved livelihoods for their daily existence. It would seem that the Tamil political leadership is working in tandem with the people's interests and their wants. The alienation of the Tamil leadership is similar to that of the southern leaders who also do not seem to be aware of the fact that most Sri Lankans no longer want confrontation.

The victory of the Tamil parties in the 2011 local government elections should not be looked upon with triumphalism, or as strengthening of the mono-culture of the Tamils or to claim that the Tamils will only vote for Tamil candidates. On the contrary, past experience has demonstrated that if appropriate policies are implemented, the deserving candidate will be supported, as it happened with the Presidential candidate, Mr. Hector Kobbekaduwa, in October 1982. Their support was a response to the successful implementation of the agricultural policy which permitted farmers in the North to net in large profits from their chilli and onion cultivations. Despite a boycott call by the TULF and other Tamil groups, the Tamils went to the polls. Mr. Kobbekaduwa received more votes than the Tamil Presidential candidate. This is a pointer to the need for non-partisan policies to gain confidence of the minorities.

## Development – The new role of the Tamil leadership in the post-war scenario.

As a first step, there is a great compulsion for the Tamil leadership to work within the available political system. Once the Provincial council in the North is set up, the Tamil leaders must initiate people-focussed programs to enhance the quality of life for the people within the shortest possible time; concentrate on the most vulnerable sections of the North and East, the internally displaced people, the war widows, the trauma patients, the disabled and the elderly, and put to effect, strategies for their welfare and upkeep. They should not be abandoned to the vagaries of time, to the hostile climate around them or to political ambitions. By working within the available system, the advantages to the people will be immeasurable. Negotiations for better options in governance can be a parallel process.

The block vote gained by the Tamil parties in the local elections is not a confirmation of a permanent role for these parties. On all accounts, the people are tired of politics and politicians and they want to move on. Soon, new blood and young leadership from within the Tamil and Muslim communities, whose memory will extend only to the war and not much beyond, will come up. It would be easier to work out compromises with them if the government plays fair and does not throw its muscle power to control the minorities that have demonstrated immense spirit and courage throughout the three decade war and thereafter. It would be a national asset to co-opt such people together and work a fair system of governance for development, growth and social welfare in the country.

Disturbingly, two years after the war, the steps for harmonious coexistence have been slow in coming and there is a lurking fear that a failure to take swift meaningful steps will create, once again, mistrust and suspicion. If we do not address the outstanding issues at the earliest, what begin as irritants will lead to serious repercussions, if not today, but at a foreseeable point of time. We should leave no room for the recurrence of the horrors of the last 30 to 40 years.

## Remove perception of state aided demographic change

The building of defence service settlements in the North and East, for purposes of security, has been perceived as a veiled attempt to change the demographic pattern of the population in the North and East. The war weary people are naturally cautious of being surrounded by service personnel, even under conditions of friendship from the cadres. The war is not a distant memory and people will need a respite before being comfortable with security forces around, certainly not as a permanent situation. It must also be noted that geographic localities cannot be intruded upon to provide economic opportunities or settlements for new populations, at least not at the initial stages, when experimentations with confidence building measures are being actively pursued. There would come a time when people would have had adequate opportunities for social change and progress to an extent when geographic locations or ethnic ratios will not matter. One can hope that national identity will take precedence over ethnic identity.

It is encouraging, that the Tamils and Muslims who wanted to escape the war, found it secure enough to move from Jaffna and the East to Colombo, to Panadura, to Gampaha, and other parts of the country. They have successfully worked out, for their well being, on their own terms, integrating with the other communities. More importantly, they have not seen the need to relocate at the end of the war. All this is taking place outside the focus of the politicians.

## The language issue

From 1956, language has been the major bone of contention. It is in the process of being worked out with an acceptable level of commitment. Sinhala and Tamil as the official languages and English as the link language is a constitutional provision. The program to have public servants gain competence in Sinhala or Tamil, as the case may be, will strengthen the language competence and increase the number of public servants capable of working in both languages. Institutes to train these officers have been set up outside Colombo and incentives have been provided to the officers.

## The North East Merger

The demand for the merger of the North and East has been put to rest with the Supreme Court decision denying the right to do so. Like the unitary structure for the state this is also an issue on which there is no room for flexibility. The minorities must accept this and move on. However, the 13th Amendment provides for Provinces to work together in areas of mutual advantage and this is an adequate substitute arrangement.

## Devolution Vs Development for Nation Building

For the past four decades, the minorities have unequivocally stated that they want a stake in governance to decide on policy, on development projects, to exercise freedom of choice, management and dissent as well as responsibility in power sharing with people's energised participation. Development alone as a substitute for devolution will be unacceptable because minorities want to be owners of the governance processes and not be mere beneficiaries.

In fact, the Provincial Councils as institutions for power sharing are part of the Constitution-is-the-law-of-the-land, from 1987. The argument that accelerated development will make devolution irrelevant will not hold. This is the type of argument that will send the minorities voting entirely on the basis of ethnicity and for secession. If the provision for devolution is abandoned as a constitutional mechanism, the country would have done a full circle and gone back to a 1956 kind of thinking. Above all, it will be a case of infringement of the Constitution. It would also be imprudent to relegate the concept of devolution as an unacceptable political formula just as federalism has been relegated to by politicians and their advisors. Except in the North, provincial councils are functioning with whatever shortcomings there may be in its construct. None of the provinces have shown any inclination to separate from the rest of the country. If equity of status to all the communities is maintained, why will the minorities want to divide?

The quotation from Amartya Sen aptly indicates the path for future moves. "Assessment of development cannot be divorced from the lives that people can lead and the real freedom that they enjoy. Development can scarcely be seen merely in terms of enhancement of inanimate objects of convenience, such as the rise in the GNP (or in personal incomes), or industrialisation, as they may be means to the real ends. Their value must depend on what they do to the life and freedom of the people involved which must be central to the idea of development". [1]

## Bill of Rights

Inclusion of a Bill of Rights to the Constitution will protect the rights of the people from infringements from the government and the bureaucracy. The bill must be entrenched so that amendments will be possible only through a referendum. The provisions, fundamental rights and provisions of the different constitutions, although comprehensive in formulation, failed to give security to the people because of the wide ranging built-in clauses that provide for restrictions on these rights and freedoms. A Bill of Rights with an entrenchment clause may perhaps be the answer.

## Constitutionally prohibit communal politics

It may be a healthy precedent to place severe strictures on communal politics in whatever form or from whomsoever it emanates. This is vital if an overarching national consciousness is to be fostered to unify the country. Soon after the '83 pogrom, the then government was quick to introduce the 6th Amendment, denying all members of Parliament, the right to advocate separation, at a time, when the call should have been for appeasement. It should therefore not be an insurmountable problem for the Rajapakshe government, with the large majority that the government commands, to introduce a bill that will prohibit, constitutionally, the espousal of divisive communal politics.

## Restore Civilian Administration in the North and East

Normalisation of conditions in the North and East would require the restoration of civilian administration. The government, quite legitimately, fears the recurrence of the separatist mindset and has therefore replaced key civilian positions with security personnel in these two areas. This is counter-productive at this point of time, as the people regard the army as an occupying force. There are less invasive ways of overseeing security threats such as the inconspicuous use of intelligence officers to the 'watch posts'.

---

[1] Amartya Sen, "The Idea of Justice", *Journal of Human Development*, Vol 9, Issue 3, 2008

The icons of the majority culture, the use of Sinhala theme names and name boards in an almost 100% Tamil area lends itself to the misinterpretation. It must be mentioned that Hindus look upon the Buddha as an incarnation of the Hindu avatars and bear no hostility to the Buddha or Buddhism. Likewise the Buddhists worship the pantheon of Hindu Gods as Devas and pray for their blessings.

## Judiciary

There is an urgent need to have an independent judiciary unfettered by the numerous manipulations of the recent past. In people's perception, the judiciary remains diminished. The judiciary must be the best guarantor of the rule of law, of the supremacy of the constitution and the values of legal and political pluralism. The independence of the system must be such that its processes can be insulated from politicization, so that both the majority and the minorities can be certain that their constitutional and legal rights will be secure. We might have to go back in time to review how it worked in the 60's, when the judiciary was considered an independent institution beholden to none, following the best principles of jurisprudence, dictated to by eminently learned and sovereign judges.

## Accelerated economic development for peaceful cohabitation.

Increasing numbers of educated, unemployed and skilled and unskilled workers seeking employment have outstripped available economic opportunities in the country. Since economic opportunities have become lean, it has unwittingly fuelled the growth of chauvinism. Consequently, class competition, again, a result of limited opportunities for individual growth, particularly among the professional middle classes becomes sharp and frustrations lead to the hardening of anti-minority positions.

Caste discrimination remains another aspect of the conflict. Being an intra- Tamil issue, this remains a contest between the traditional elites and the depressed communities who are poor and downtrodden. Improved education and increased access to economic opportunities will give the depressed communities, the leeway to emancipate themselves from the strictures of a caste ridden society as well as to exploit opportunities that come their way.

Development would need large infusion of capital and diversification of the economy, through planned participatory initiatives that will bring the heart and soul to this process as opposed to the cerebral top down development.

## Nation building and Development with a proactive diaspora.

The Tamil diaspora must become proactive in the reconciliation process and refrain from espousing the cause of Eelam as it is detrimental to the confidence and trust building environment. This is true of the Sinhala Diaspora too, who should now begin to think of building the nation within a clearly recognised plural polity. It will be necessary to reach out to those among the diaspora, who are willing to work with Sri Lanka, as a commitment to their kith and kin in the task of bringing about sustainable reconciliation to this traumatised nation. Their linkages to the North and East and their strengths in the financial and intellectual resource base should be used to develop the war torn areas and give the people the necessary opportunities for personal and community advancement. The provinces must also be encouraged to attract investments from outside, channelled through the Central Bank but without permitting any attempt by the Centre, to cash in on any part of the investment that is received directly by the provinces. This will activate the participatory process and create the opportunities for the use of local capacity at all stages of the programs and in the absence of local capacity, introduce projects for capacity building as part of a long term planning.

## Education

There is a need to create opportunities for the educated mass of people. The authorities must give priority to infrastructure, quality upgrading of teaching skills, access to knowledge, information systems, equitable distribution of resources throughout the country etc. with special focus on restoration of the destruction to the educational facilities in the North and East.

## Post war Role for the media as peace builders.

The media in Sri Lanka has to become self consciously conscientious about the post war requirements - to build peace and put the disparate blocks of contentious viewpoints together, to form a symmetrical whole. The media has a major 'informational role' and a scrupulous effort must be made to use its extensive news coverage, to bring a truthful account to the table and bring responsible reporting to its readers, to help in healing, in building trust and in building the nation modelled on the principles of justice. To this effect, the reporters must become investigativors and search for information that will contribute to the above objectives. It is the duty and the obligation of the media to disseminate objectively, ways and means of putting the communities together by publicising any of the shortcomings that need to be highlighted for corrective steps, building awareness of the constructive measures taken and by driving home the need for uniting the people as one nation.

The pre- war practice of sections of the media to rabble rouse communal ill feeling has to be a thing of the past since the whole country has suffered from consequences of the war. It matters not who the owners of the media may be, truth must be sacred and obligation to the country must be predominant; all other obligations must be secondary at this moment in history.

## Civil Society

Finally, the role of civil society cannot be underestimated. Mass mobilisation and empowerment of civil society has to be undertaken to enthuse the citizens towards a future in a plural society. Taking the peace process forward has to be the responsibility of citizens working in their own communities. A cohesive nation cannot be built from a top down process, it must be generated, from within, with institutions designed to bring neutrality in the administration of the ethnic diversity and effective enforcement of the rule of law.

There are many civil society efforts at peace making and reconstruction of the North and the East.

The trail to Jaffna, by two young men from the corporate sector, has set ablaze, a long line of connectivity throughout the stretch of the walk, from the South to the North, undertaken to collect funds for a cancer ward for children in Jaffna. The enthusiasm with which people from the rural areas all along the way parted with their rupees and cents, with many evocations of merit on those who participated, is heartening. This is indeed a demonstration of empathy towards the Tamils, an eye opener to the leadership who fear repercussions from the south and central Sri Lanka.

This must also help the Tamil parties to look upon rapprochement as the only way to the resolution of their concerns.

A UK based charity called Oru Panai -one pot- has set up a branch in Sri Lanka to provide nutritious mid-day meals to 22,000 school children, covering 175 schools in Mullaitivu, Mannar, Vavuniya and Jaffna. A survey was made to assess the situation and the choice made on the basis of information gathered from it. An Ex Corporate CEO is the chairman and two physicians act as secretary and Treasurer. All three officials are drawn from the three different communities, deliberately constituted to reflect unity of purpose, by the group. A registered charity with the Ministry of Justice, it is supported by the World Food Program.

A concert was held on the 3 September, 2011 organised by a former Ambassador, together with a church group, to raise funds for rebuilding the North and the East. The music was by artists from the Sinhala and minority communities and within the hall, there was a solid feeling of togetherness.

Another fund raiser for children in the north will be held in October, in London, by the lady who organises for charity, annually. The concert was titled, "symphony for a child". There are many others who are running programs without the general public being aware of their interest in peace building.

Civil society has taken the initiative and it is hoped that these moves will convince the government that people bear no ill-will towards the minorities and that progress towards uniting the country is taking place at the civil society level, even if they are small efforts.

What we need is inspiring, enlightened and bold leadership that can cut across any opposition if the leadership knows the direction that has to be taken. The poem *Invictus* was written by William Ernest Henley and Nelson Mandela quotes the following lines from it:

I am the master of my fate

I am the captain of my soul.

This kind of confidence is what Sri Lanka must have from her leaders.

# Harmonising Ethnic Diversity: Linguistic Challenges

**11**

N. Selvakkumaran

## Introduction

**B**eing a multi-ethnic, multi-religious and multi-lingual country, Sri Lanka's experience in harmonising ethnic diversity has not been a success story since independence in 1948. Even before independence, signs of disharmony showed up when the Soulbury Commission visited the country to find out the views of natives with regard to grants of responsible governments to the locals. Instead of taking steps to harmonise ethnic diversity in the post independent Ceylon, the successive governments were engaged in actions, in the fields of citizenship, franchise and use and recognition of languages, which represented divisive approaches to nation building. Both legislative and executive actions of the governments failed to promote unity and harmony; instead they were seen to display a sense of exclusion and disrespect. The judiciary in the post independent Ceylon too failed to live up to the expectations of the makers of the Constitution.

Language plays a major role in the life of a person, community and country. In addition to being a tool to gather and transmit knowledge, to communicate thoughts, ideas and information to others, to share ideas and feelings with others, language forms an important element in the identity of an individual. It not only binds individuals as a community or group but also is inextricably intertwined with one's culture and identity. Failure to recognise a person's right to use his or her own language to transact business and failure to facilitate the recognition and identity of the person through the use of his or her language have led to many a problem in many countries.

There is no doubt that the non-recognition as well as non-implementation of linguistic rights of minorities have contributed, in a significant way, to the ethnic conflict in the country. This also led to an environment in which people speaking different tongues could not understand each other; mistrust and misunderstanding grew in place of goodwill and harmony amongst these people who belonged to different communities. In addition, a feeling of being culturally and ethnically relegated due to one's language and furthermore a sense of being denied opportunities of employment in the public sector have contributed to the deterioration of ethnic relations in the country. These have, amidst others, paved the way for the breakdown of good relationships amongst the different ethnic groups and led to the civil war in the country.

Language rights are recognised as human rights and they form part of cultural rights recognised by international instruments.[1] In Sri Lanka too, they are expressly and implicitly recognised as fundamental rights under the present Constitution, though the recognition has come after causing great damage to the good relations that existed amongst the communities in the country.

## The Post-Independence Era

The fundamental law of the land - the Independence Constitution[2] which was not enacted in the native languages but in the English did not refer to the use of any languages specifically; nor was there any reference to an 'official language' in the Constitution. But an implied reference to language rights under the Ceylon (Constitution) Order in Council was discernible from

---

[1] Refer to the UN Declaration on the Rights of Persons belonging to National or Ethnic, Religious and Linguistic Minorities, 1992, International Covenant on Civil and Political Rights, 1966, the International Covenant on Economic, Social and Cultural Rights, 1966 and the Universal Declaration of Human Rights, 1948.

[2] This consisted primarily of the Ceylon (Constitution) Order in Council, 1946, the Ceylon (Independence) Order in Council, 1947 and the Ceylon Independence Act, 1947 made by the British authorities.

Section 29, which provided that -

(1) Subject to the provisions of this Order, the Parliament shall have power to make laws for the peace, order and good government of the Island.

(2) No such law shall –

   (a) Prohibit or restrict the free exercise of any religion; or

   (b) Make persons of any community or religion liable to disabilities or restrictions, to which persons of other communities or religions are not made liable; or

   (c) Confer on persons of any community or religion, any privilege or advantage which is not conferred on persons of other communities or religions;

(3) Any law made in contravention of subsection (2) of this Section shall, to the extent of such contravention, be void.

It was clear from paragraphs (b) and (c) of Sub-Section 2 of Section 29 that the Constitution did not confer upon the Parliament the plenary legislative power to make laws which discriminated one community vis-à-vis other communities. In effect, it prevented the legislature from making laws which are, amongst other things, discriminatory on linguistic grounds. Section 29 (3) made those provisions of any law which contravened Section 29 (2) void.

Sensing some untoward turn of events, Dr. N. M Perera, Member of Parliament for Ruwanwella, proposed a private members' motion, in October 1955, to the effect that "the Ceylon (Constitution) Order in Council should be amended forthwith to provide for the Sinhalese and Tamil languages to be State languages of Ceylon with parity of status throughout the Island."[3] Dr. Perera explained what he meant by parity of status in the course of his

---

[3] Parliament of Ceylon, Hansard, Vol.23, Cols.572/573.

[4] Parliament of Ceylon, Hansard, Vol.23, Cols.610/611.

speech. He stated that "parity of status means recognition of a right that each individual has to be governed in the language he understands."[4]

Even in the absence of any specific express references to language rights as such, the constitutional prescription contained in the Independence Constitution clearly laid out the framework within which language policy should have been adopted by the government. However, later events – legislative, executive/administrative and judicial – were not consonant with this framework. The first legislative blow to the linguistic equality recognised in and guaranteed by the Independence Constitution came to pass when the Parliament, soon after the General Election in 1956 passed the Official Language Act, No. 33 of 1956, which was popularly referred to as the Sinhala Only Act. The concept of official language did not enter the constitutional and legislative domain until the enactment of this Act, which in its preamble stated that it was "an Act to prescribe the Sinhala Language as the one Official Language of Ceylon and to enable certain transitory provisions to be made".

The events that took place thereafter, in the country, made the Government enact the Tamil Language (Special Provisions) Act No. 28 of 1958, which permitted *"the use"* of the Tamil language. Through the preamble of the Act, the Parliament of the day made it clear that the use of the Tamil language was not to conflict with the provisions of the Official Language Act of 1956. The Tamil language was not accorded the status of Official Language, nor were the people, whose mother tongue was Tamil, given the same rights as those whose mother tongue was Sinhala. The Tamil language was only permitted to be used, but without any elevation or recognition as an Official Language. The Act permitted the use of Tamil as a medium of instruction, as a medium of examination for admission to the Public Service, for correspondence between officials and members of the public or between any local authority in the Northern and Eastern Provinces and any official and for some prescribed administrative purposes within those provinces.[5]

---

[5] It is from 1966 only that Tamil has been used as the language of administration in the North and East. See Paragraph 2.1, Chapter II of the Memorandum of Recommendations of the Official Languages Commission, June 2005.

The validity of the Official Language Act of 1956 was called in question when a Tamil public servant filed a case against the denial by the government to pay him increments because he had not passed the Sinhala proficiency examination prescribed by the Treasury Circular No. 560 of 1961 under the Act. His main argument was that the Act was void as it was ultra vires Section 29 (2) of the Constitution. The District Court held with the Plaintiff holding that the Act was ultra vires. The Attorney General appealed against the judgment of the District Court, to the Supreme Court. The appeal court overturned the decision of the original court on the ground that under our law, a government servant was not entitled to enforce the terms and rules governing the public service by going to court. The appeal court in this country did not go into the question of constitutionality of the Official Language Act.[6] While holding against the judgment of the Supreme Court, the Privy Council sent back the case to the Supreme Court, in Sri Lanka, for its decision on the constitutionality of the impugned Act. The Privy Council also did not decide that question itself.[7] When the case came back, the events had overtaken it and the 1972 Constitution came into existence and prevented any court from going into the question of the validity of any laws.

## Under the First Republican Constitution, 1972

The concept of Official Language was given constitutional recognition by the First Republican Constitution in 1972, for the first time in the country. The Constitution elevated the Official Language Act, 1956 and the Tamil Language (Special Provisions) Act, 1958 by according constitutional recognition to them.[8] The Constitution did not incorporate an express anti-discrimination provision, similar to Section 29 (2) & (3) of the Independence Constitution, though it contained an Article on Fundamental Rights that included 'the right to equality' in general terms. However, all the existing laws were expressly stated to be in force and valid, until they are altered or annulled by the National State Assembly under the Constitution. The cumulative effect of these constitutional provisions was to make the validity of the Official Language Act and the Tamil Language (Special Provisions) Act unassailable by the courts.

---

[6]The Attorney General vs. Kodeeswaran [1967] 70 N.L.R.121.

[7] Kodeeswaran v. The Attorney General [1969] 72 N.L.R 337.

[8] Articles 7 and 8 of the Constitution of Sri Lanka (Ceylon), 1972.

The 1ˢᵗ Republican Constitution for the first time dealt with three different matters having an impact on the linguistic rights of people of the country separately.[9] Titled "Language", Chapter III of the Constitution dealt with (a) Official Language, (b) Language of Legislation, and (c) Language of the Courts.

Accordingly,

(i)  The Official Language of Sri Lanka shall be Sinhala as provided by the Official Language Act, 1956 and the use of the Tamil language shall be in accordance with the Tamil Language (Special Provisions) Act, 1958.

(ii)  All laws shall be enacted in Sinhala and there shall a Tamil translation of them.

(iii)  The language of the courts and tribunals shall be Sinhala throughout Sri Lanka and their records including pleadings, proceedings, judgments etc., of all judicial and ministerial acts shall be in Sinhala.

The National State Assembly could make laws to provide for differently for the North and East, in this respect. In the North and East, a person may submit his pleadings, applications, etc in Tamil and participate in the proceedings in Tamil. The court was required to cause a Sinhala translation for the purposes of the record. Every party, judge, juryman not conversant with the language used in a court, shall have the right to interpretation and to translation into Sinhala or Tamil as the case may be. Similarly such a person could obtain any record which he or she was entitled to obtain, in Sinhala or Tamil. The Constitution authorised the Minister of Justice, with the concurrence of the Cabinet of Ministers, to issue orders, directions permitting the use of a language other than Sinhala or Tamil, to a judge.

One of the significant developments that took place after the 1972 Constitution was that the laws were enacted by the National State Assembly in Sinhala and they had translations in Tamil as well. There was a translation in English also, though it was not specified as a requirement in the Constitution. This allowed the ordinary Sinhala and Tamil speaking people

---

[9] Chapter III, titled Language of the Constitution of Sri Lanka (Ceylon) 1972.

to have access to the laws of the country in their mother tongues, though the Tamil version was only a translation and the Sinhala text was the official version.

## Under the Second Republican Constitution, 1978

The Second Republican Constitution expressly and implicitly recognised linguistic rights of people as fundamental rights, in addition to a Chapter on Language. Language rights are inseparable from the fundamental right of freedom of thought.[10] One of the grounds on which discrimination cannot be permitted is language.[11] Similarly a person charged with an offence has a right to be heard at a 'fair' trial by a competent court[12]; and if a person is tried in a language which he or she does not understand, the trial cannot be said to be a fair one, unless there is reasonable interpretation of what transpired at the trial. In terms of the 1978 Constitution, every citizen is entitled to the fundamental right of freedom of speech, expression including publication and freedom to enjoy and promote his or her own culture and to use his or her own language.[13] One of the directive principles of state policy declared by the Constitution is that 'the State shall assist the development of the culture and the languages of the People'.[14] Another directive principle requires the State to ensure equality of opportunity to citizens so that no citizen shall suffer any disability on the ground of language, amongst others.[15] These provisions in the constitutional chapters on 'Fundamental Rights'[16] and 'Directive Principles of State Policy and Fundamental Duties'[17] clearly recognise the linguistic rights of the people in the country.

On the question of Official Language of the country, the 2nd Republican Constitution of 1978 did not depart from the position under the 1972

---

[10] Art. 10 of the 2nd Republican Constitution of Sri Lanka, 1978.

[11] Art.12 of the Constitution of 1978.

[12] Art. 13 (3) of the Constitution of 1978.

[13] Art. 14 of the Constitution of 1978.

[14] Art. 27 (10) of the Constitution of 1978.

[15] Art.27 (6) of the Constitution of 1978.

[16] Chapter III of the Constitution of 1978.

[17] Chapter VI of the Constitution of 1978.

Constitution. It made the Sinhala language, the Official Language.[18] However, having continued with the concept of official language, the Constitution introduced[19] the concept of National Languages which are said to be Sinhala and Tamil. The Constitution also expanded the scope of language rights by making specific provisions in many fields. Accordingly, the Constitution has specific provisions relating to -

  (i)  language of legislators,

  (ii)  language of legislation,

  (iii)  language of administration,

  (iv)  language of communication,

  (v)  language of examination,

  (vi)  language of education/instruction, and

  (vii)  language of the courts.

## Under the Second Republican Constitution, post 13th and 16th Amendments

Pursuant to the Indo-Sri Lanka Accord, the 13th Amendment was enacted to the Second Republican Constitution. While the primary objective of the 13th Amendment was to introduce a sub-national level government viz., the Provincial Council system, in the country, it also dealt with the linguistic rights of the country's minorities. It amended Article 18 of the Constitution that dealt with the Official Language of the country. Although there was an obvious grammatical error in the amendment effected to Article 18, Tamil was also made an official language. The amended Article 18 reads as follows:

Article 18. (1) The Official Language of Sri Lanka shall be Sinhala.

     (2) Tamil shall also be an official language.

     (3) English shall be the link language.

---

[18] Art.18 of the Constitution of Sri Lanka, 1978.

[19] Art 19 of the Constitution of Sri Lanka, 1978.

(4) Parliament shall by law provide for the implementation of the provisions of this Chapter.

The 13th Amendment did not amend any other constitutional provisions in the Chapter on Language other than Article 18. The significance of the 13th Amendment with regard to languages spoken in the country was that it gave the Tamil language, for the first time in the constitutional history of this country, the status of Official Language. Article 18 introduced also a new concept of 'link language' in the country without any explanation as to its significance or implications. The link language is English. One had to wait for the 16th Amendment to the Constitution to understand what the purpose and functions are of the designated link language.

On the face of the 13th Amendment, it could be claimed that it gave parity of status to both Sinhala and Tamil as the Official Languages. One would have felt that by this Amendment, both Sinhala and Tamil would be the Official Languages of the entire country and would be used so in the entire country. There was a clear inconsistency between the amended Article 18 and other Articles in the Chapter on Language and the failure to amend the other constitutional provisions on Language to bring them in line with the newly given status of the Tamil language, left room for lack of clarity. It should be noted that the mere designation of the Tamil language as an official language did not in reality mean anything for practical purposes. Although Article 18 (4) provided that the Parliament shall, by law, provide for the implementation of the provisions of the Chapter on Language, the Parliament did not enact any law towards this end until 1991, save the 16th Amendment in 1988.

The 16th Amendment to the Second Republican Constitution, 1978 introduced several changes to the then prevailing position on languages. Articles 22 and 23 of the Constitution were replaced and Articles 20 and 24 were amended. A new Article 25a was introduced. These changes represent the present position. This Amendment empowered a Member of any Provincial Council to perform his or her duties and discharge his or her functions in the Provincial Council in either of the National Languages. This right was also enjoyed by a Member of Parliament and any local authority.

The substituted Article 22 declares that Sinhala and Tamil shall be the languages of administration throughout Sri Lanka. It further states that Sinhala shall be the language of administration and be used for the maintenance of public records and the transaction of all business by public institutions in all the provinces of Sri Lanka, save the Northern and Eastern Provinces. With regard to the North and East, Tamil shall be the language of administration and be used for the maintenance of public records and the transaction of all business by public institutions. Therefore, having given the Tamil Language the status of being an official language of the country, its use as a language of administration has been restricted to the North and East. In effect, the constitutional amendment reinstated more or less the position that was obtained under the Tamil Language (Special Provisions) Act of 1958. The parity of status supposedly extended by the Thirteenth Amendment was thus short lived.

However, a proviso, which has been added to Article 22 (1), is a progressive one. On the basis of the proportion which one linguistic minority within an AGA's division has, to the total population of the area, the President may direct that both Sinhala and Tamil or a language other than the language used as the language of administration in the province, be used as the language of administration for such area. It must be noted that no percentage is specified and the discretion lies with the President. This provision envisages that all governmental institutions within that AGA's division will be operational, bilingually.

The 16th Amendment also provided that in an area where Sinhala is used as the language of administration, a person, other than an official acting in his or her official capacity, is entitled to receive communication and transact business with any official in either Tamil or English. On the other hand, where he or she is entitled to receive copies of or extracts from official register, record, documents or publication, he or she is entitled to receive such a copy or a translation thereof in either Tamil or English and to receive any document or translation thereof, which is executed by any official for the purpose of being issued to him or her in either Tamil or English. In the case of an area, where Tamil is the language of administration, a person is entitled to receive the above in Sinhala or English. This provision is drafted in a convoluted and confusing manner. This provision may lead to an absurd position of a Sinhala speaking person, in an area where Sinhala is the language of administration being told that he or she is entitled to receive communication in either Tamil or English. The reverse is said to apply to a Tamil speaking person in an area where Tamil is the language of administration.[20] Art. 22 (2) In any area where Sinhala is used as the language of administration, a person other than an official acting in his official capacity, shall be entitled:

(a) to receive communications from and to communicate and transact business with, any official in his official capacity, in either Tamil or English;

(b) if the law recognises his right to inspect or to obtain copies of or extracts from any official register, record, publication or other document, to obtain a copy of, or an extract from such register, record, publication or other document, or a translation thereof, as the case may be, in either Tamil or English;

(c) where a document is executed by any official for the purpose of being issued to him, to obtain such document or a translation thereof, in either Tamil or English.

(3) In any area where Tamil is used as the language of administration, a person other than an official acting in his official capacity, shall be entitled to exercise the rights, and to obtain the services, referred to in sub paragraphs (a), (b) and (c) of paragraph (2) of this Article in Sinhala or English.

---

[20] Art. 22 (2) In any area where Sinhala is used as the language of administration, a person other than an official acting in his official capacity, shall be entitled:

(a) to receive communications from and to communicate and transact business with, any official in his official capacity, in either Tamil or English;

(b) if the law recognises his right to inspect or to obtain copies of or extracts from any official register, record, publication or other document, to obtain a copy of, or an extract from such register, record, publication or other document, or a translation thereof, as the case may be, in either Tamil or English;

(c) where a document is executed by any official for the purpose of being issued to him, to obtain such document or a translation thereof, in either Tamil or English.

(3) In any area where Tamil is used as the language of administration, a person other than an official acting in his official capacity, shall be entitled to exercise the rights, and to obtain the services, referred to in sub paragraphs (a), (b) and (c) of paragraph (2) of this Article in Sinhala or English.

The latter position must have resulted as an oversight of the draftsman who would have been concentrating on protecting the rights of the linguistic minorities in the areas where the language of administration is the other official language.

While the 16th Amendment permits a member of the public in any part of the country to correspond with government departments and officials in the language of his choice and receive communication in Sinhala/English or in Tamil/English, a person in his official capacity is not entitled to correspond or receive correspondence in his mother tongue when the language of administration of the area is not his mother tongue.[21] The said Amendment makes it clear that if there happens to be any inconsistency between the provisions of any law and those of the Chapter on Language, the provisions of the Chapter should prevail.[22]

## Enforcement of Linguistic Rights

The present Constitution provides for judicial remedy against any infringement or imminent infringement of language rights and fundamental rights recognised in the Constitution by executive or administrative action. The Supreme Court has been vested with sole and exclusive jurisdiction in this regard. Although the Constitution lays down restrictive conditions relating to the legal standing of an applicant as well as the time period within which he or she should come before the Supreme Court, the power of the Court to grant relief is very wide. It has the power to grant such relief or make such directions as it may deem just and equitable in the circumstances of each case.

This apart, the Human Rights Commission of Sri Lanka established under the Human Rights Commission of Sri Lanka Act No. 21 of 1996, has also been given power to entertain complaints relating to infringements or imminent infringements of fundamental rights by executive or administrative actions. As some of the linguistic rights have been recognised in the Constitutional provisions on fundamental rights, they could be the subject of inquiry by the Commission. However, the Commission can make

---

[21] See Art. 36 (1) of the Constitution of the Republic of Sri Lanka Bill, August 2000 which did not have the qualifying phrase 'other than an official acting in his official capacity'.

[22] Art.25 (a) of the Constitution of 1978. See s.5 of the Sixteenth Amendment.

recommendations and those recommendations are not of enforceable nature like the judgments of the Supreme Court.

The Parliamentary Commissioner for Administration, an office established by the 1978 Constitution too has authority to investigate and report upon complaints of infringement of fundamental rights and other injustices by public officers and officers of public institutions and local authorities.[23]

## Official Languages Commission Act No. 18 of 1991

Mandated by the amended Article 18 of the Constitution, Parliament passed the Official Languages Commission Act No. 18 of 1991. The enactment of the above Act was a step towards ensuring the effective implementation of the languages policy contained in the Constitution. The following form some of the general objects of the Commission:

(a) To recommend principles of policy, relating to the use of the Official Languages and to monitor and supervise compliance with the provisions contained in Chapter IV of the Constitution;

(b) To take all such actions and measures as are necessary to ensure the use of the languages referred to in Article 18 of the Constitution, in accordance with the spirit and intent of Chapter IV of the Constitution;

(c) To promote the appreciation of the Official Languages and the acceptance, maintenance and continuance of their status, equality and right of use; and

(d) To conduct investigations and to take remedial action.

The Commission has a variety of powers to ensure the implementation of the provisions of the Constitution, relating to languages. These include, amongst others, the power to –

(a) initiate reviews of any regulations, directives, administrative

---

[23] Art. 156 of the Constitution of 1978

practices, which affect or may affect the status or use of any of the relevant languages;

(b) issue or commission such studies or policy papers on the status or use of the relevant languages as may be deemed necessary or desirable;

(c) undertake such public educational activities, including, sponsoring or initiating publications or other media presentations, on the status or use of the relevant languages as it may consider desirable;

(d) do all such other things as are necessary for or incidental to, the attainment of the objects of the Commission or necessary for or incidental to, exercise of any powers of the Commission.[24]

The Commission has the power to investigate complaints arising from any act or omission in the administration of the affairs of any public institution relating to the status and use of any of the relevant languages. Towards the investigation of complaints, it has the power to summon witnesses and compel the production of documents. The Act also provides for taking judicial action in Provincial High Courts against the failure to implement any recommendations made by the Commission. Similarly any wilful failure or neglect in transacting business in a particular relevant language, by a public officer, can be the subject to prosecution in a Magistrate Court.

The Official Languages Commission and the Ministry of Constitutional Affairs and Ethnic Integration have been instrumental in getting two important administrative circulars[25] issued by the Ministry of Public Administration in 2007. One circular deals with incentives to officers who secure language competency in the second official language in addition to the language of their entry to the public service. The other Circular makes it mandatory to every officer joining the government service after the 1st of July 2007, to gain competency in the second official language within a period of five years under the threat of being not confirmed in the post if he/she does not obtain the proficiency.

---

[24] Section 7 of the Official Languages Commission Act, 1991

[25] Public Administration Circulars Nos. 3 and 7 of 2007.

These are welcome moves by the Commission though there is a lot more to be done with regard to enforcement and monitoring. The human capacity and financial resources of the Commission are woefully inadequate compared with the enormity of duties cast on it. The Commission should be given adequate human and financial resources as well as power to set up regional level sub-commissions to discharge its functions at such levels.

## Conclusion

The unsatisfactory state of affairs of the implementation of the Tamil language as an Official Language in the Districts other than those coming under the Northern and Eastern Provinces was aptly captured by a former Chairman[26] of the Official Languages Commission when he commented that "there is an enormous gap between constitutional provisions and their application". Attributing the possible reason for this situation, he observed "that successive governments have failed to fully implement the policy as laid down in the Constitution, which calls for a bilingual administration at all levels and throughout the country...". There is a lack of sensitivity to recognise and respect the linguistic rights of the people whose mother tongue is Tamil but who are citizens of this country. Also it was recognised that there was a lack of initiative to implement the Tamil Language as the official language of the country, though it was recognized to be so in 1987.

A critical evaluation of the developments of the linguistic rights of the people whose mother tongue is Tamil, unmistakably reveals, that their rights have been recognised very grudgingly but incrementally. However, this is done after creating a sense of relegation with regard to the status of the language in the minds of those people in the mid nineteen fifties. This has had a decisive effect on the ethnic relations of different communities in the country, since 1956. Even though attempts were made to rectify the situation and to reverse it, in 1987, the telling effects of the ill-conceived, unfortunate and monumental policy decision taken in 1956 does still continue to afflict the ethnic relations of the communities in the country. So much so that although changes effected by constitutional amendments have neutralised officially, the effect and purport of some of the legislation on the status and use of languages in the country, the restrictive and discriminatory pieces of

---

[26] Public Administration Circulars Nos. 3 and 7 of 2007.

legislation such as the 'Sinhala Only' Act, 1956 and the Tamil Language (Special Provisions) Act, 1958 have not been 'repealed and removed' from the statute book yet.

It is, however, to be noted that the recognition of collective right of the majority community cannot be criticised as it upheld and recognised the linguistic rights of the majority people of the country. However, what was unacceptable and unwise was the fact that only one of the native languages was made the official language while the other was relegated to an inferior status and the denying of the minority linguistic community of its language right. This was perhaps propelled by political expediency to ride to power overnight. Thereafter, administrative convenience and political expediency have been dictating the incremental 'grant' of language rights to the linguistic minorities in the country. The constitutional, legislative and administrative developments of language rights have not been driven by a desire to approach the issue from a rights-based perspective. Political opportunism and administrative expediency have been the main reasons for the present parlous state of the implementation of linguistic rights of the minorities.

Although successive governments have taken steps to address the concerns of linguistic rights of all people in the country through statutory and constitutional enactments, with regard to the use of languages, the implementation of these policy pronouncements has not been effectively and efficiently carried through. The main reason for the inefficient and ineffective implementation of the Official Languages Policy is the fact that the National Policy on Recruitment to the Public/Provincial/Judicial Service and the National Policy on Education/Higher Education do not go hand in hand with the Official Languages Policy. In fact these policies and the strategies of policy implementation undermine the Official Languages Policy as reflected in the Constitution. Unless there is a concerted effort to synchronise these three in order to work towards achieving a common objective, the lack of proper implementation will continue to bewilder this country. That will, in turn, make the task of harmonising ethnic diversity in this country, a distant reality and a perpetual challenge.[27]

---

[27] Views and expressions contained in this chapter have already been made by the writer in some of his earlier works.

# Contributors

**Brig K Srinivasan (Retd)** is a defence and security analyst, who, while in service, has been involved in addressing internal conflicts in Jammu and Kashmir. At Centre for Security Analysis, he guides and supervises the work of research fellows. His areas of interests include conflict analysis & peace building, disaster management and the role of civil society in conflict situations. He is an active member of the working group on non-traditional security of Regional Network of Strategic Studies Centres, set up by NESA Centre, National Defence University, Washington.

**Ms Ancy Joseph** is a research assistant at the Centre for Security Analysis, Chennai. She has written articles on the conflict and the current affairs of Myanmar as well as on internal conflicts in South Asia. As a Research Assistant at CSA, she assists the Executive Director in carrying out the Centre's programs and projects. She holds a Master of Philosophy Degree in Public Administration and Masters Degree in International Studies and Public Administration from the University of Madras.

**Prof Tissa Vitharana** is currently the Senior Minister of Scientific Affairs in the Sri Lankan Government. He is also the General Secretary of the Lanka Sama Samaja Party. Prof. Vitarana is visiting Professor of Microbiology, Faculty of Medical Sciences, University of Sri Jayawardenapura. Prof. Vitharana obtained his MBBS and M.D. in Ceylon and obtained his Ph.D from the University of London in virology. He is a member of several Select Committees in the Parliament e.g. Electoral Reforms Committee, Committee to amend the 17th Amendment to the Constitution etc. He was also the

Chairman of the All Party Representatives Committee (APRC) – mandated to produce a set of political proposals, as the framework for a new Constitution, to facilitate the peace process and solve the National Question in Sri Lanka.

**Ambassador G Parthasarathy** is a retired Foreign Service Officer. He possesses a B.E. Degree in Electrical Engineering, from the College of Engineering, Guindy, Madras. He has served as Ambassador of India to Myanmar, 1992-95, High Commissioner of India to Australia 1995-98, High Commissioner of India to Pakistan 1998-2000 and High Commissioner of India, Cyprus 1990-92. In New Delhi, Amb Parthasarathy was Deputy Secretary in the Foreign Secretary's Office 1976-1978. He has served as Spokesman, Ministry of External Affairs and Information Adviser and Spokesman in the Prime Minister's Office with Prime Minister Rajiv Gandhi 1985-90. He has been a member of the Indian Delegations in several international conferences, including summits at United Nations, Non-Aligned Movement and SAARC. He is currently a visiting Professor in the Centre for Policy Research in New Delhi. He is also Visiting Professor for International Relations in the University of Punjab, Chandigarh and a Senior Fellow at the Centre for Strategic and International Studies in New Delhi.

**Prof Rajiva Wijesinha** is currently an advisor on reconciliation, to H.E., the President of Sri Lanka and a member of Parliament. He obtained his MA in classics and D Phil in English from Oxford University. Until most recently, he was the Senior Professor of languages at the Sabaragamuva University of Sri Lanka. From 2007-2009, he was the Secretary-General of the Sri Lankan Government Secretariat for Coordinating the Peace Process (SCOPP) and from June 2008 to February 2010, he also served as the Secretary to the Ministry of Disaster Management and Human Rights. Prof. Wijesinha is the author of numerous publications, both fiction and non-fiction, on the themes of English language & literature, English education and Sri Lankan & South Asian Politics.

**Dr Kandiah Sarveswaran** obtained his M.A in Political Science and PhD in South Asian Studies from the Jawaharlal Nehru University in New Delhi, India. He is currently a visiting lecturer at the University of Colombo,

Departments of Political Science and International Relations. He has also been a senior lecturer and coordinator of the Master's programs in Conflict and Peace Studies and Human Rights at the University of Colombo. He has authored and published extensively on the topic of Sri Lanka's conflict and peace process.

**Ambassador Javid Yusuf** is an Attorney at Law who has served as Sri Lanka's Ambassador to Saudi Arabia as well as Senior Advisor to the late Minister Lakshman Kadirgamar, during his second tenure as Foreign Minister. He has worked extensively in the field of Human Rights and Conflict Resolution including as a Member of the National Human Rights Commission and a Member of a Presidential Commission that inquired into high profile Human Rights violations. A Civil Society activist with wide experience and serving on the Boards of Management of several Civil Society Organisations, he has been very active in the field of media as well. Having functioned as the first Head of the Peace Secretariat for Muslims, he has also served as Principal of Zahira College, Colombo.

**Dr Saman Kelegama** is the Executive Director of the Institute of Policy Studies of Sri Lanka (IPS). Prior to this appointment as the Executive Director, he was a Research Fellow at the IPS from 1990-1994. He obtained his doctorate - D.Phil (Econ) from Oxford University, UK in 1990. He has an MSc (Econ) from Oxford University and MSc (Maths) from the Indian Institute of Technology (IIT), Kanpur, India. He was a Government of India Cultural Scholar for his undergraduate studies during 1978-1983. He was a Visiting Fellow at the South Asia Research Centre, Australian National University, Canberra, Australia (1998); Government of India Distinguished Visiting Scholar (1998); Salzburg Fellow (1997); USIS International Visitor (1993); and Visiting Fellow, Institute of Social Studies, The Hague, The Netherlands (1992/3). He has been a Visiting Lecturer at the University of Colombo, Post-Graduate Institute of Management (PIM), Sri Lanka, Bandaranaike Diplomatic Training Institute (BDTI), Sri Lanka and several other institutions. He has served as a consultant to the World Bank, ADB, UNDP, UNIDO, ILO, UN-ESCAP and the Commonwealth Secretariat. Currently, he is a Fellow of the National Academy of Sciences of Sri Lanka.

**Mr S.B. Divaratne** is currently the Secretary of the Presidential Task Force for Resettlement, Development and Security in the Northern Province. Mr. Divaratne is a retired Senior Sri Lanka Administrative Service Officer and joined the service in 1971. He has held positions of Addl. Secretary: Ministry of Samurdhi, Rural Development and Sports, Commissioner, Co-operative Development, Director General, National Budget, Ministry of Finance, Deputy Secretary to the Treasury and Commissioner General, Essential Services. He possesses a B.A degree from Sri Lanka and a post graduate diploma in Economics and Social Policy Planning from the University of Manchester.

**Dr N Manoharan** did his M.Phil and Ph.D on South Asia from the School of International Studies, Jawaharlal Nehru University. He has over 15 years of research experience. He was South Asia Visiting Fellow at the East-West Centre, Washington (2005) and recipient of the prestigious Mahbub-ul Haq Award (2006) for his research. His areas of interest include internal security, terrorism, Sri Lanka, Maldives, human rights, ethnic conflicts, multiculturalism, security sector reforms and conflict resolution. His recent publications include *India's War on Terror* (New Delhi: Knowledge World, 2010) (Co-edited), *SAARC: Towards Greater Connectivity* (New Delhi: Shipra, 2008) (Co-edited); *Ethnic Violence and Human Rights in Sri Lanka* (New Delhi: Samskriti, 2007); *Counterterrorism Legislation in Sri Lanka: Evaluating Efficacy* (Washington D.C.: East-West Centre, 2006). His forthcoming books are *Counter-terror Laws and Security in Developing Democracies: Lessons from India and Sri Lanka, Sri Lanka: A Conflict Dictionary, India-Sri Lanka Relations: So Far, So Good and 'Security Deficit': A Comprehensive Internal Security Strategy for India.*

**Ms Gnana Moonesinghe** is Founder Director of Shramaya, an NGO, which finances micro initiatives to increase the earning capacity of the poor in selected areas in Kalutara and Colombo districts. She has been a Researcher at the Marga Institute and has held the positions of Secretary and Vice-Chairperson in South Asia Partnership (SAP) 1985 – 1995. She has been a Board member of Sri Lanka Canada Development Fund (SLCDF) from 1990 – 1995. Ms. Moonesinghe possesses a B.A degree in Political Science from the University of Peradeniya. She is a freelance contributor to newspapers and journals and is the editor and author of several publications, titles etc. which include *Towards Nation Building in Sri Lanka (1993), Build a Bridge (2005) – Five short stories based on the theme of violence in Sri Lanka, Nation Building: Priorities for Sustainability and Inclusivity (2011).*

**Mr N Selvakumaran**, LL.B. (Hons) (Colombo), M.Phil (Colombo) and Attorney-at-Law, is the Dean, Faculty of Law, University of Colombo. He was previously Co-Director of the Centre for Policy Research and Analysis (CEPRA), University of Colombo and a member of the Sri Lanka Human Rights Commission and the Chairman of the *Commission* of Official *Languages.*

# CSA Publications

**Conflict Resolution and Peace Building**

- ▶ Conflict Resolution and Peace Building in Sri Lanka
- ▶ Federalism and Conflict Resolution in Sri Lanka
- ▶ Peace Process in Sri Lanka: Challenges & Opportunities
- ▶ Conflict over Fisheries in the Palk Bay Region
- ▶ Conflict in Sri Lanka: The Road Ahead
- ▶ Peace and Conflict Resolution: Emerging Ideas
- ▶ From Winning the War to Winning Peace: Post War Rebuilding of the Society in Sri Lanka
- ▶ Internal Conflicts in Myanmar: Transnational Consequences
- ▶ Internal Conflicts in Nepal: Transnational Consequences
- ▶ The Naxal Threat: Causes, State Responses and Consequences
- ▶ Conflict in Sri Lanka: Internal and External Consequences
- ▶ Conflicts in North-East: Internal and External Effects
- ▶ Conflict in Jammu and Kashmir: Impact on Polity, Society and Economy

## Security Studies

- US and the Rising Powers: India and China

- Maritime Security in the Indian Ocean Region: Critical Issues in Debate

- Public Perceptions of Security in India: Results of a National Survey

- Essential Components of National Security

- Economic Growth and National Security

- Security Dimensions of India and Southeast Asia

- India & ASEAN: Non-Traditional Security Threats

- Emerging Challenges to Energy Security in the Asia Pacific

- Security Dimensions of Peninsular India

- Socio-Economic Security of Peninsular India

## Civil Society and Governance

- Civil Society and Governance in Modern India

- Civil Society in Conflict Situations

- Civil Society and Human Security: South & Southeast Asian Experiences